Withypool

The Story of an Exmoor Village

Richard Westcott

Editor Victoria Thomas

With newly commissioned photographs and an accompanying village archive CD-ROM edited by Chris Chapman

SKERRYVORE PRODUCTIONS

Published in 2014 by Skerryvore Productions Limited

Copyright © Skerryvore Productions Limited

a Skerryvore production 2014

South Molton
Devon EX36 3AN

www.skerryvoreproductions.co.uk
skerryvoreproductions@gmail.com

ISBN 978-0-9931039-0-2

All rights reserved. No part of this publication may be reproduced, stored in a retrieval system, or transmitted in any form or by any means without the prior permission of the copyright holder.

Front cover photograph by Jo Minoprio

Printed by Short Run Press Ltd, Exeter, Devon

Ashley and Jo Down, Lanacre. Photograph by Chris Chapman

Dedication

'*The dogs bark, but the caravan moves on*' is an Arab proverb which aptly describes how, in holding these lands, the generations of lords of the manor have been enabled to enjoy life – their lives – in this wonderful parish.

This book attempts to encapsulate the progress of the 'caravan' through history, illuminate the pleasures of Withypool and recognise the hard work of generations of the community who have created the way of life enjoyed by so many.

When the dogs bark next our caravan will move on to Louis Down, and it is to him and his generation that this book is dedicated.

Travel well.

Lanacre
December 2014

Acknowledgements

We have been overwhelmed by the welcome and generosity shown to us in our endeavours to gather material for this book.

First, we are very grateful to the South West Heritage Trust and to the Exmoor Society for our use of their archives and libraries. In particular we pay tribute to the *Exmoor Review*, thanking past editors and contributors for their work in amassing such a rich resource for anyone making a study of any aspect of Exmoor. Hope Bourne's perceptions have been invaluable.

Many people have given us their time and welcomed us into their homes, telling us stories and showing and lending us personal papers, photographs, pictures and possessions, which have helped enormously. We have not been able to include everything but we are very grateful and hope that there may be an opportunity at a later date to gather this rich collection into a village archive. It would be impossible to name everyone who has helped, so we ask forgiveness for anyone not listed here.

Our thanks are due to: Jenny Acland, Gwen Bawden, Joan Bidie, Jake Blackmore, John and Doone Chatfeild-Roberts, Edna Clatworthy, Mary Davies, Edna Hayes, Bruce Heywood and family, Tony Howard, Rosalie Hughes, Margaret Hutchings, Gillian Lamble, Tim and Marian Lloyd, Luke Martineau, the Milton family, Lindy Mitchell, Bob and Jacqueline Patten, Di Pershouse, Steven Pugsley, Mike and Gina Rawle, Mary Rayson, the Robinson family, Beryl Scoins, Jill Scoins, Doris Sloley, Julian and Polly Soltau, Sue and Ted Wakeham, Rita Westcott, Pat and Charlie Williams, Sybil Williams, Michael and David Witney and June Zeitzen.

We are especially grateful to Barbara Adams, Wendy Davey, Millie Edwards, Margaret Hankey and Shirley Scoins whose support, advice and help enabled us to write this book.

Above all, we thank Ashley and Jo Down for their initiative, encouragement and support throughout, without which this book would never have been started, let alone finished.

Any mistakes or shortcomings are entirely ours; we apologise for the inevitable inaccuracies which will have occurred, and for any offence caused either in omission or commission.

Contents

Introduction		vii
Preamble		viii
Chapter 1	Through Pre-historic Mists . . .	1
Chapter 2	From Pre-history to Royal Forest	7
Chapter 3	Royal Forest	13
Chapter 4	Medieval Times	19
Chapter 5	The Manorial Courts of Withypool and the Manor at Lanacre – *by Christopher Chanter*	27
Chapter 6	Later Medieval Times	39
Chapter 7	Towards Modern Times	43
Chapter 8	The Nineteenth Century	51
Chapter 9	The First Half of the Twentieth Century	60
Chapter 10	The Second Half of the Twentieth Century	75
Chapter 11	Natural Withypool	83
Chapter 12	Around the Village	89
Chapter 13	Past, Present and Future – People and Place	119
Chapter 14	Postscript	122

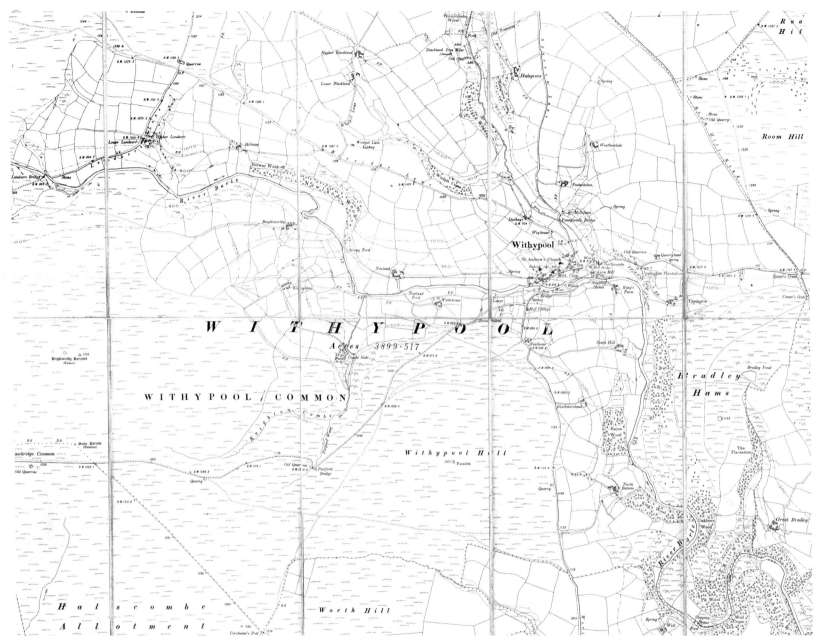

Ordnance Survey map of Withypool. © Crown Copyright 1902

Introduction

This is the story of a little but ancient place, nestling in its fold of Exmoor – a quintessential Exmoor village, whose story not only represents an intriguing local history but also reflects national events in English history.

Our story begins in the mists of pre-history and concludes with living voices. It draws on original resources along with well-told stories, and hopes to be both serious and scholarly as well as amusing and entertaining.

It is therefore a book for all – for those who have lived here all their lives, often with many a generation preceding them, as well as for those others who have arrived more recently, not to mention anyone with a local or passing interest in the village as a happy place to visit. In short, it is a book for all those who know and love Withypool.

Chapter 5, which forms the important central section of the book, draws on some fascinating original material. The Lanacre manorial documents, dating back to 1772, have a very interesting story to tell in their own right – the comings and goings, payments and non-payments, doings and misdoings which were dealt with locally and recorded beautifully on vellum.

These documents which have hardly seen the light of day, let alone been fully studied and annotated, give a fascinating insight into how justice was administered and local administration was managed in times past. It was partly the growing awareness of the importance of these records that stimulated the family who now live at Lanacre to commission this book.

Landacre Bridge. Photograph by Jo Minoprio.

Preamble

Withypool is near the centre of Exmoor National Park and the parish covers 7,653 acres with a population of about 200. The civil parish, known as Withypool and Hawkridge, includes the village of Hawkridge, but the present book focuses on the settlement of Withypool.

The village lies across the Barle Valley, with the river flowing through its centre. From the east, the river Barle approaches Lanacre between Bradymoor to the north, and Brightworthy to the south, each crowned by their prehistoric artefacts, winding its way towards the settlement, with the land levelling.

Moorland gives way to the green fields of the farms of Blackland, Brightworthy, Knighton, Newland and Waterhouse, although the moor still comes close to the south as Withypool Common.

Here in the centre of the village the now shallow Barle runs through the arches of the bridge, with houses on either side, welcoming shop and tea room, squat-towered church and meeting of roads.

Whether you are a visitor or local, it is hard not to stop for a moment, as so many others have for so many centuries past, to chat – for there is always someone here – or simply rest awhile and enjoy the sense of peace and place.

The river continues on its way, past more houses, Kings Farm, the Royal Oak and the old mill, to swing south down a lovely valley, with the Two Moors Way following its east bank and Withypool Hill now to the west. Past South Hill the trees draw closer, and the Barle, heading now towards Tarr Steps, leaves the village, en route to neighbouring Hawkridge.

Withypool may be a small settlement then, in terms of population, but in other respects it is a large place. Here we find a great variety of landscapes, like Exmoor itself – of which it may be considered a microcosm – from open moor (complete with wonderful ancient remains) to green pastures, from a rushing river to quiet habitations, from deep woods to still waters.

It therefore comes as no surprise to learn that this area, all this lovely valley through which the Barle flows, has been recognised as a Site of Special Scientific Interest so that it enjoys special protection.

Above all here you will find a quiet and reassuring feeling of gentle, natural activity, often positively inspirational. Such happy ruminations are not just ours – many others have been equally moved to reflect in such terms, ranging from a president of the Royal Academy to a president of the United States, from a world famous novelist to our own Hope Bourne.

So let us begin . . .

Early morning looking east to Withypool Hill. Photograph by Chris Chapman.

Chapter 1

Through Pre-historic Mists . . .

'Withypool is situated on the banks of the Barle at that point where the big river leaves the confines of the high hills to flow for a space between wide and fertile meadows, before again other hills and thick woods close in upon it as it hurries southward. All around lies the moor: northwards and eastwards the great mass of the Forest and the Commons beyond, southwards the Withypool, Anstey and Molland moors, eastwards the high heather of Winsford Hill . . .' (1)

Hope Bourne's characteristically clear and well modulated description places Withypool precisely. Perhaps, she acknowledged, she was prejudiced, but for her – and many would echo this – there is none so truly a village of Exmoor as Withypool.

Unlike the other high moors of the south-west, Exmoor is not granite. Exmoor is softer, subtler. Exmoor is made of older sedimentary rocks, dominated by shales, slates and sandstones deposited over a period of 50 million years which began some 400 million years ago, south of the equator, in tropical climes (2).

There followed tremendous movements such as the wonderfully named Variscan Orogeny with uplifting, contortions and erosions to produce, finally, the gentle but deeply folded landscape with its many running waters, beside one of which Withypool nestles.

The parish sees the meeting of morte slates with Pickwell Down Beds (felsite and tuff). Or put more simply, as in *Kelly's Directory*, 'the soil is shillet and peat, and the subsoil rock.'

The ecclesiastical parish of Withypool covers a wide area of moorland, extending beyond Lanacre in the north-west, to Brightworthy Barrows in the west, and to Comer's Cross in the east.

We cannot be sure when the first people came to roam the hills and valleys of Withypool, no doubt hunting deer, spearing fish, cracking hazel nuts and sampling berries and fungi (3). But it was probably long before the Atlantic tides, pushing up channel, finally cut this island off from the continent, round about 6000BC.

After this a moist and warm climate helped afforestation by oak, alder, lime and elm, alongside the hardy pine and hazel of earlier years. Drier times followed, leading into the later Mesolithic, or Middle Stone Age. Exactly who, where and how many people may have been living in the Withypool area at this time remains controversial, but it must have offered then, as now, an agreeable spot with its shelter, fresh water and good hunting.

Certainly an 'almost perfect' stone circle on Withypool Hill was set on a gentle south-west facing slope, probably in late Neolithic times. The story of the discovery of this 36 metre diameter circle by Archibald Hamilton's horse stumbling over one of its stones in 1898 is well known – and reminiscent of other archaeological discoveries.

Whybrow, who considered it to be the best of the Exmoor stone circles (4), explains how it lies slightly to the south of the saddle running south-west from the summit of the hill, and not to the north as shown on the maps, which was why 'many people, following the maps, fail to find the circle.' He reckoned that there were probably originally about 100 stones here, but that only between 30 and 40 were left.

Later scrupulous examination by the staff of the Royal Commission on the Historical Monuments of England (RCHME), published in 1992 and presented by Riley and Wilson-North in *The Field Archaeology of Exmoor*, shows the detailed configuration.

Whybrow found himself disappointed when he compared this structure to Stonehenge or Avebury, or even to some of the Dartmoor circles, but this is an inappropriate comparison. These Exmoor stone settings – modest, quiet and softly spoken – remain nonetheless 'almost without parallel in Britain and Ireland' (Burl, quoted in (5)).

Some may find them un-dramatic but these earliest works of man represent his first enduring marks upon the land. Depleted, with individual stones often obscured, almost forgotten in the fortunate absence of signings, fencing and explanatory apparatus – here they still are.

Amongst these extraordinary sites Withypool's circle is a very special monument. After thousands of years their achievement is that they remain – with their quiet questions that we cannot answer, and their statements that we cannot hear. Modern man stands in this isolated place, unsure and chastened.

How was this circle made? Who were the people who made it? Did they have special roles; how many of them were there; how long did it take; in which season and at what time of day was it done; were there earlier versions, as at Stonehenge and other monuments? Is the centre of this circle special?

Imagine a simple compass of a line staked in a particular spot by an individual, the end being drawn round to trace out a circle. Many people are probably present, perhaps whole families, possibly each with their own stone, all of which are small, and some very small, talking to each other in a tongue totally incomprehensible to us now.

What did they do then? How was the circle used as time passed? When, why and how was it abandoned?

And the most important question of all: what was it for?

As these questions remain unanswered, feelings of respect – even, strangely, affection and kinship – well up. Who cannot feel humbled contemplating such questions in this special place?

Near Portford Bridge is a large mound-field, including a cluster of three probable ring barrows, which spreads across the saddle of a low ridge running from Green Barrow towards the stone circle. The association of the dip of this saddle with the headwaters of the Portford stream, and nearby a 'good slab of stone about three feet high' removed during road alterations in the 1920s, as remembered by Fred Milton, give grounds for one authority to view this area as one considered 'especially holy' (3).

With that barrow on the summit of Withypool Hill, the two crowning Brightworthy, Green Barrow above the

The 'almost perfect' stone circle on a south-western slope of Withypool Hill gives us a glimpse into the lives of the peoples of the late Neolithic and Early Bronze Age. Even though the size of the stones themselves may be unimpressive, Withypool's stone circle commands distant views to the south-west and south-east and could possibly have been a place for gatherings and religious ceremony or a form of observatory to mark the winter solstice. Photograph by Chris Chapman.

An aerial shot of Cow Castle, an Iron Age fort, upstream from Landacre Bridge on the Barle, which links the presence of Celtic tribes all along the river, through Withypool down to Mounsey Castle and Brewer's Castle towards Dulverton.
Photograph by Chris Chapman.

Lanacre trough quern. The trough-shaped quern stone found in the river below Lanacre dates from around 5,000 to 3,000 years ago and was used by early settlers to grind corn. It may originally have come from the pre-historic settlement recently discovered at nearby Bradymoor. Photograph by Chris Chapman.

head of Knighton Combe and the Bradymoor barrow, Withypool is surrounded by at least five barrows. These round barrows may be seen as the earliest works of man, his first enduring marks upon the land. Their makers may have been nomadic, living in tents and moving with the seasons. Although we know little for sure, we may safely say that a thoughtful, constructive and organised people lived and had their being here.

A recent interesting discovery near Landacre Bridge, dating from some 5,000 to 3,000 years ago, is a quern stone used for grinding corn. The pleasing trough shape of the stone caught the observant eye of a passer-by, who thought it might make an attractive bird-bath and took it home.

Subsequent archaeological examination suggested that it was a hollowed-out basin in which corn was ground using a small hand held stone called a rubber. It may be that this useful implement relates to the recently discovered settlements a little upstream to the north on Bradymoor. These south-facing, well-drained and watered slopes might well have made an agreeable site for those earliest farmers with their grinding stones and other tools. It is thought that the quern stone might have rolled down the hill into the river below and, with the passing millennia, eventually washed down to the bridge area below Lanacre.

We do know that the people of the New Stone Age, who built many a barrow on hilltops across western England and Wales, brought livestock and seed for crops, and understood ploughing and pottery (3).

It would be easy, after glancing at what survives of their implements like the grinding stone, to minimise their technical achievements.

But with their symbolic awareness of thresholds and

transitions, as reflected in their passage graves, and their complex agenda for these very carefully constructed circles, of which there is such a fine example here, we have to give them credit for a high level of intellectual searching and even sophistication.

We must stand before such artefacts – whether a stone basin or hilltop barrow – with respect and some humility.

Neolithic people cut down the natural forest for firewood, for building and to clear land for cultivation in successive patches. When the soil was exhausted, settlements such as the one at Withypool would have become extended and further established.

And as the climate began to deteriorate around 1200BC, there was a further incentive for families to move downhill for shelter, perhaps to gather in the centre of what was to become Withypool.

We cannot be certain, but there must have been some degree of specialisation by now, with a variety of skills from hunting to farming, from making pottery to spinning and weaving.

So as we move from pre-history into the beginnings of recorded times we can imagine a settled, perhaps almost prosperous, group of people scattered across our site. It is not yet 'Withypool', of course, but undoubtedly the precursors of the community that was eventually to develop into the more formal settlement of Saxon times. The careful construction of the circle alone suggests a degree of attachment, if not permanence.

There were to be many more arrivals (arrivals, then as now, met with suspicion, and sometimes fully justified fear) as well as departures, as we shall see. But it is not too far-fetched to imagine that some small genetic element of those people might live on in some of today's inhabitants of Withypool.

References

1. Hope Bourne, *A Village of the Moor*, Exmoor Review, 1966, No. 7, p. 45
2. Paul Pickering, *The Geological Foundations of Exmoor*, Exmoor Review, 1997, Vol. 38, p. 81
3. Hazel Eardley-Wilmot, *Ancient Exmoor*, The Exmoor Press, 1983, p. 7 and p. 25
4. Charles Whybrow, *Antiquary's Exmoor*, p. 11, The Exmoor Press, 1970
5. Hazel Riley and Robert Wilson-North, *The Field Archaeology of Exmoor*, English Heritage, 2001

Chapter 2

From Pre-history to Royal Forest

Towards the end of the Bronze Age, as the climate deteriorated, people began to come down from the high uplands into more sheltered valleys such as the site of Withypool. Then another – possibly linked – change in the population occurred: the arrival of Iron Age Celts.

The earliest of these settlers seem to have blended peaceably but later competition for land seems to have led to bloodshed (1). What conflicts may have taken place by the Barle in this now tranquil village can only be imagined, but the brooding presence of the several hill forts overlooking our river suggests that there was need for protection.

The resourceful Celtic people, who with the earlier inhabitants became known as the Dumnonii, eventually settled down, becoming competent farmers and capable craftsmen. It has been suggested that it was during the last century BC that the first isolated farms appeared (2).

Exmoor's diverse and dissected landscape favours dispersed settlement as the settlement pattern of today shows (5). Obviously 'Welsh' names, like those elsewhere on Exmoor, such as Triscombe and Treeborough, are less evident in the Withypool area but there are of course several 'combes' (from the Celtic 'cwm') in the parish, and at least some of the existing settlements may have begun as Celtic farmsteads.

We can imagine a group of huts, one larger to accommodate the chief with his precious cattle and horses, surrounded by a palisade, with some small enclosures for the growing of crops and the pounding of animals.

'The land for the most part would still be an unclaimed waste of moorland, scrub, and thick oak, ash and beech forest. Hill farming, from the very first, would be almost entirely pastoral. The wealth of the farmers and of the community lay in cattle, and all the pattern of farming and the cycle of the year would revolve around the beasts . . .' (2)

Iron production was another important part of their skills. It is always difficult to date the earliest workings in mines when overlaid by later workings, but it is interesting to think that Blackland may have seen some quarrying at this time. In any event, their trading activities, including that valuable iron, seemed to have enabled them to come to sensible arrangements some 500 years later, at the time of the arrival of the latest invaders, the Romans.

The traditional view that the successful invasion of AD43 brought the various Celtic peoples, including our Dumnonii, into the civilised world needs reconsidering.

Hope Bourne's drawing of a Bronze Age encampment from *A Little History of Exmoor* is rich in detail.

To start with, Julius Caesar's first invasion of 55BC with nearly nearly 100 ships provoked a rapid and effective response from the Celts using horses, chariots and javelins.

Caesar counted the Celts as Gaullish and described them as brave fighters and clever tacticians. They were able to use the alphabet and were sufficiently well organised into a hierarchy that was ruled by a priestly Druidical class (3). We have to make an effort to remind ourselves what skills and resources, competences and culture must have underpinned the lives of the men and women who lived here before the Romans arrived.

That said, there followed nearly four centuries of Roman rule. How much this was to be felt in our particular part of Exmoor is questionable. There were two small observation posts – hardly forts – on the north coast, to be sure. Snell claims that Roman coins were picked up at Brendon and Exe Head, but such finds prove no more than that valued objects have often been gathered up and carried to another place. He also dismisses other traditions such as the westward march of Ostorius's Legion, concluding that there is no real evidence that the Romans penetrated further west than the Quantocks (4).

In Eardley-Wilmot's opinion 'the conqueror's network of roads and forts seems to have passed east, west and south of the misty hills, not across them' (3). More recent authorities seem to acknowledge that, with the discovery of Roman coins at Dulverton, and radiocarbon dating from workings at Sherracombe, 'the Romans took an active interest in getting what they could from Exmoor', while recognising that 'the arrival of the Romans is not well told by Exmoor's landscape' (5).

The settlements at Withypool can hardly have been affected by these latest invaders. We may picture a continuing life of agricultural, pastoral and craft activity, no doubt intermittently disturbed but essentially quietly concerned with subsistence in poor weather and modest progress in fairer times. Perhaps therefore no-one in Withypool would have noticed the departure of the Roman legions in the 5th century AD.

But those imperialists left behind lasting changes. They had brought a new and civilising religion in the later years of the empire. In those hundreds of years the indigenous people, even in the middle of Exmoor, had been altered. We may or may not see them as Romano-Britons but they had been exposed to Christianity, and the Caratacus inscription on a longstone on nearby Winsford Hill is written in 5th or 6th century Latin lettering not in the Celtic alphabet Ogam (3).

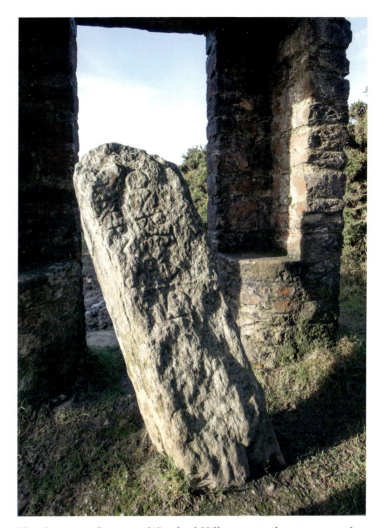

The Caratacus Stone on Winsford Hill suggests the presence of the Romans on Exmoor. Theories differ as to whom the stone was dedicated, but it is thought to indicate the site of a grave. Photograph by Chris Chapman.

Discussion about the Caratacus stone and to whom it was dedicated still continues. Older theories suggest connections with the heroic leader of the Silures, from the other side of the estuary, who 'fought long and hard

The Barle valley in spring as the beech trees come into leaf. Photograph by Jo Minoprio.

against the Romans, but at last fell into their hands and was exhibited by the Emperor Claudius in AD51' (4).

Later, the idea that the name corresponded to 'Carantaci' linked it to a holy man who was a contemporary of King Arthur and who gave his name to Carhampton where he was said to have built an oratory.

Nowadays it is thought that, while the stone probably indicates the site of a grave, its position close to a former ridgeway suggests that it was sited to be clearly visible to passers-by (5).

For a while, perhaps 200 years, Exmoor's people continued their pastoral existence: 'it is generally assumed that the Roman retreat from Britain would have gone unnoticed by the ordinary people in the south west' (5). But new invaders were pressing in from at least two directions, and – following trade routes – people were leaving the area for Armorica, soon to be named Brittany for this very reason.

Irish and Welsh missionaries were arriving with their own brand of Christianity. So, although Withypool is some way from the coast to the north, and from the front of advancing Saxons to the east, repercussions must have been felt even in our little isolated settlement.

As so often in the Dark Ages, with such little evidence of any sort, we find ourselves reduced to guesswork. Were there bloody battles? Were whole families terrorised into fleeing from their patches? Or was there a more gentle drift? Did the small settlements quietly and simply evolve into the more recognisable farms, hamlets and organised field systems we associate with the medieval period?

We do know names of a few shadowy kings such as Constantine, Cadwy and Geraint (5). We know that there was a major battle in 682 when the Britons were scattered by the Saxons and that Geraint, King of Dumnonia, was decisively defeated in 710 (6). But after this we hear no more of battles (2).

By about 720 the west country as far as the river Tamar was in Saxon hands. Although perhaps deep in the combes, high up on the moor and hidden away in desolate parts of Exmoor a Celtic resistance burnt low, if not bright. Why otherwise would Ine, the Saxon King of Wessex need to build a new fortress in Taunton?

The Barle valley through beech trees. Photograph by Jo Minoprio.

As before, we can only speculate about our settlement by the Barle in this new Saxon kingdom. Certainly, there are many Saxon names all around – the Leys, Worths and Worthys, the Lands, Lades and Tons.

And the name of our settlement? Withypool is thought to derive from Widepolle, meaning willow pool, as found in the Domesday Book. Although the word that the Normans used was itself of Saxon origin – *withig* meaning willow.

In summary, most would now agree that (leaving aside for the moment its outlying farmsteads) our village of Withypool is a Saxon settlement, more or less properly established between the 7th and 9th centuries (7).

Further disturbance struck in the 9th century. Viking longships were soon to come round Land's End, penetrate the Bristol Channel and invade the north coast. Fortunes swung this way and that, but in 878 they were defeated 'with great slaughter'. Although the battle – perhaps at Countisbury – was some way from Withypool, news of this threat and bloodshed must have percolated down through Exmoor, especially with the various raids that followed.

By the end of the 10th century these attacks subsided but battles raged elsewhere between Saxons and Danes, leaving the Dane Cnut King of most of what was now England.

Viking names are nowhere to be found on Exmoor so we may assume that the good people of Withypool quietly carried on, relatively undisturbed. But most authorities now agree that it was at this time that Exmoor developed its most enduring and important role, a key determinant of Withypool's future; it was to become a Royal Forest.

References

1 Roger Burton, *The Heritage of Exmoor*, R A Burton, 1989, p. 20
2 Hope L Bourne, *A Little History of Exmoor*, J M Dent & Sons, 1968, p. 20
3 Hazel Eardley-Wilmot, *Ancient Exmoor*, The Exmoor Press, 1983
4 F J Snell, *A Book of Exmoor*, Methuen & Co, 1903, p. 5
5 Hazel Riley and Rob Wilson-North, *The Field Archaeology of Exmoor*, English Heritage, 2001, p. 81
6 E T MacDermot, *The History of the Forest of Exmoor*, Barnicott & Pearce, The Wessex Press, 1911
7 Hope Bourne, *A Village of the Moor*, Exmoor Review, 1966, p. 45

Chapter 3

Royal Forest

So what would our landscape have looked like in these latter years of the first millennium, as we move towards the Norman Conquest of 1066? We would see a scattering of settlements on the higher ground where the soil was good and the site well-watered and sheltered – a good example being Higher Blackland.

'Long, long ago some sturdy Saxon settler came up to the hill, and saw that it was good, and laid his hand upon it, and set the first rooftree upon it, cast up earthen banks, for the first little fields, and broke the heather for the plough. "Blackland" means heather ground, and a heather hill it must have been . . .' (1)

It takes a self-sufficient character like Hope Bourne to convey some of the determination, ingenuity and sheer doggedness that underpinned the achievements of these pioneers.

But it was on the lower ground that most of the farms were to be found, for carving out a place was generally easier on the edge of the wilderness. As the settlements grew, more land was cleared and enclosed with the high and wide banks of earth and turf for which the Saxons were noted, and in their little fields corn and other crops were grown (1).

In the summer the cattle and sheep were driven up on to the old rough pastures to be brought down again to winter on the farms, and this began a custom that has carried on for more than 1,000 years. It facilitated the process whereby the Saxon kings began to appropriate all the land not in continual use by the farming communities.

As much of this land was either too steep or wet to plough, or the soil was too thin, there was little competition to own land on Exmoor so Saxon settlement was confined to preferred areas. These settlers established fuel and grazing rights over the nearer parts of the moor, which through usage came to be known as 'rights of common', but made no attempt to advance into the interior (2). So the wastelands became the king's deer and game reserves, and from that the Royal Forest.

A circular process ensured that as unclaimed land came into the king's possession his power grew, ensuring that more unclaimed land came to be regarded as royal property. As the important rights of common, such as summer grazing and peat digging, were to be recognised by the Normans and subsequently went on to play a crucial role in Withypool's history, we will look at them in more detail later.

Hope Bourne's drawing of Saxon settlers building a farmstead, from *A Little History of Exmoor*, deserves close attention. For example, on the left-hand side of the picture, the wooden gate being made is not just any gate but distinctively Exmoor in style.

The preservation of the king's rights over the Royal Forest, essentially as a game reserve and royal hunting ground, created a need for specific and, as time went on, strong protection. So a legal system appeared called forest law.

Anglo-Saxon and, later, Anglo-Danish kings developed this prerogative – 'King Canute was a mighty hunter, and would without doubt have been glad to claim any land with an abundance of deer as a private hunting-ground for himself' (1). But it was the Norman kings who increased the areas and reinforced their protection with a definitive system developed in the reign of Henry II.

Hinds crossing the River Barle to Bradymoor. In Saxon times between the 5th and 11th centuries the wastelands of Exmoor became the king's deer and game reserves, and so evolved into the Royal Forest. Photograph by Chris Chapman.

For now it may be helpful to recognise three important factors in play (3). Firstly, inside the forest the common law was suspended. Secondly, the commoners wanted to retain their fuel and grazing rights and also prevent any extension of the forest boundaries, and thus of forest law. Thirdly, the king wanted to extend – or at least preserve – the boundaries of the forest to maximise his use and income.

These tensions underlay much of the developments over the following centuries with a fluctuating boundary reflecting varying fortunes.

Royal forests were not necessarily wooded. It was forest law that defined them as 'a definite tract of land within which a particular body of law was enforced, having for its object the preservation of certain animals *ferae naturae*' (4). However, some authorities recognise that 'covert for deer is essential to a forest' (6).

On the issue of afforestation Hamilton writes in 1907 (6) 'With the exception of a few quite modern plantations, there are not, and probably never were, within the bounds of the forest of Exmoor, as determined by the perambulation of 1298, any woods at all, and this is specifically stated in an affidavit filed in 1622 . . . "There are no woods nor copses other than one oake called Kite Oake and a few thornes growinge here and there . . . nor any other shelter for deere other than sedgebusshes, rushbusshyes, fearnes, heath or such like."'

Nonetheless, until the end of the 13th century the wooded valley of the Barle from Withypool to Castle Bridge was within the forest, which was therefore not entirely destitute of woods (4).

The significance and importance of the establishment of the Royal Forest to Withypool will become clearer as we follow the history of our village.

It is in the aftermath of the Norman Conquest in 1066 that we encounter the first documentary evidence relating to Withypool. William the Conqueror, wanting to know exactly what he possessed and what dues and taxes he might therefore expect to enjoy, sent commissioners into every part of the country to make detailed reports of the lands, stock and people. We see ownership transferred from Anglo-Saxon to Norman time and again.

For the most part new Norman landowners (the church and churchmen, along with barons) took the opportunity to gather up smaller holdings into large new estates.

The Royal Forest is not formally included in the Domesday Book, that great inventory of all these assessments. There was no need, as it was already considered to be in the personal and continuing ownership of the king. So, although we read that before the conquest Widepolle had been held by three foresters, Dodo, Almer and Godric as 'four ploughs', it was now held by Robert de Olberville as theignland. This meant that its 'ownership' – essentially stewardship – was dependent on providing military service to the king on demand.

In effect Withypool was, like the rest of the Royal Forest, owned by the king. Poor old Dodo was also stripped of other land he owned, such as Worth and Westwater, farms of today on the south-east edge of Withypool (6). There is only one case of a pre-conquest owner retaining his ownership, where Ulf continued to hold Hawkwell. Otherwise it is, as Hope Bourne remarks, a pitiful tale (7).

De Olberville or D'Auberville or D'Odburville, described as one of William's servants, must have ended up as a powerful man of great substance. His original occupation is not clear but other servants of William who were granted land in Somerset include Hugh Butler, the king's cup bearer, John the porter, Ansger the cook and another Ansger who was hearth keeper. Whatever this particular adventurer had been before, he now found

Ancient plough marks are clear to see on Bradymoor. Photograph by Chris Chapman.

himself holding the office of royal huntsman and later the even more important office of master of the game (6).

Withypool assumes some importance as we follow the ownership of these offices down the years for Robert de Olberville's lands at Withypool, together with the hereditary forestership, were subsequently given to one William de Wrotham who seems to have been the king's chief forester for all the forests in Somerset and Dorset.

And what else may we learn about Withypool as it was in 1085 from the Domesday Book?

The 'four ploughs' gives some idea of the agricultural potential of the village. A hide was the average amount of land an eight-ox team could plough in an average season, which in midland or lowland countries became standardised at 120 acres, but was of course less in other parts.

A ploughland (carucate) is considered the same as a hide, which in our hill country would have been more like 40 acres. A further complication is the point that the 'four ploughs' probably represents the total area of land *capable* of being ploughed, regardless of the amount which might be tilled in any one season – in short, the entire land of the estate less the steep cleeves.

So we could imagine late 11th century Withypool as a settlement with perhaps 160 cultivated acres, surrounded by quite prosperous farms whose ownership was worthy of documentation. They were in the hands of a powerful and aspiring adventurer, noted by the king's administrators and protected by the special legislation of the Royal Forest.

References

1. Hope Bourne, *Two Exmoor Farms*, Exmoor Review, 1967, Vol. 8, p. 74
2. S H Burton, *Exmoor*, Hodder & Stoughton, 1966
3. S H Burton, *Exmoor Royal Forest in the Middle Ages*, Exmoor Review, 1966, Vol. 7, p. 52
4. E T MacDermot, *The History of the Forest of Exmoor*, Barnicott & Pearce, The Wessex Press, 1911
5. H Riley and R Wilson-North, *The Field Archaeology of Exmoor*, English Heritage, 2001, p. 90
6. A Hamilton, *The Red Deer of Exmoor*, Horace Cox, 1907, p. 153
7. Hope Bourne, *A Little History of Exmoor*, J M Dent & Sons, 1968, p. 39

Chapter 4

Medieval Times

By the beginning of the 13th century the Royal Forest was well established but there were to be many changes. Magna Carta in 1215 saw a reduction in its size, with Withypool as well as some other parishes excluded. However, by about 1400 Exmoor Forest had found the area it was to occupy for the next 300 years or so – an uninhabited stretch of moorland roughly equivalent to the present day parish of Exmoor (1).

After 1400 the crucially important way in which Withypool, now outside the true forest boundary, developed its own forest law arrangements will be considered in depth in the next chapter but the background needs to be considered here.

The most characteristic method of cultivation in medieval England was the open field system, in which the village community worked large unenclosed fields using strip allotments. Each farmer had a certain number of long narrow strips, which were not necessarily next to each other so there was often no need for hedging or fencing.

As turning the plough was cumbersome, the farmer would maximise the length of his ridge and furrow as long as was practical. These long lines, faithfully followed over the centuries and inscribed in the landscape as a living reminder of the travails of many long-forgotten generations of Withypool farmers, remain visible on the slopes around the village. Looking at the shadows of these strips one can only feel respect for the achievements wrought with such simple technology. Chris Chapman's photograph of Bradymoor in Chapter 3, page 17, shows the ancient plough marks are still clearly in evidence.

So who was living in our village in the 1400s?

There was a hierarchy with defined classes. We have already described some of the landowners – the lord of the manor – who may not have been resident. Below him were his tenants who paid rent. This was the most prosperous group: the freemen.

Next came the villeins, the people of the 'ville', who constituted the largest group, being the peasant farmers. They provided payment in kind. Although the villeins lived on and worked their 'own' land, under the feudal system various services were required, ranging from work on the lord's land to military and other duties.

A lower class of smallholders, the bordars, were of lesser means. Their holdings may have been too small to

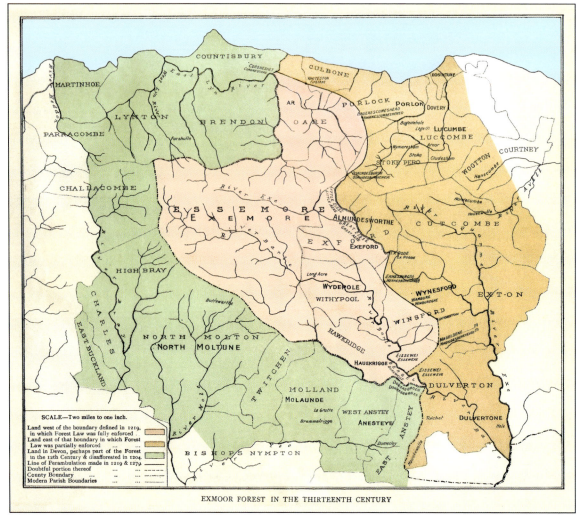

A map of the Royal Forest in the 13th century, in which Withypool can be seen to be within the boundary.

support a family so they probably supplemented their incomes by working as part-time labourers for others (1). In Withypool there were more bordars than villeins – woodsmen, herdsmen and huntsmen often employed by the royal foresters with others working as craftspeople such as smiths, carpenters, masons and shoemakers – all of whom would have needed a smallholding (1). Below them was a lower class of serfs, bondmen who enjoyed even less freedom.

Everyone, however, continued to use the waste land – that is, the common. But owing to the expanding population and the wish of lords of the manor to develop their land and make the most of their assets, the use of the common became formalised. The archaic Norman

A map of the Royal Forest in 1301, showing Withypool now 'disafforested' – that is, lying outside the forest boundary along with several other parishes.

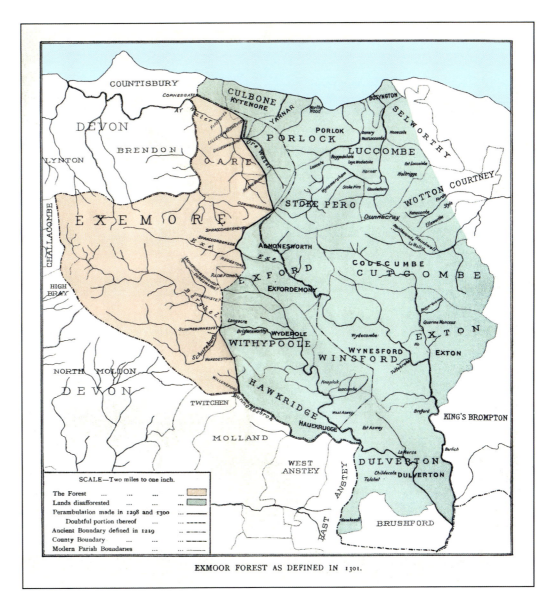

EXMOOR FOREST AS DEFINED IN 1301.

legal terms of that regulation survive, such as herbage (grazing), pannage (grazing pigs), piscary (right to fish), estovers (right to take fallen timber), turbary (right to cut peat) and commons in soil (right to quarry stone) (2).

As the Royal Forest itself was subject to common rights held by surrounding manors, such as Withypool, all this called for careful administration. This was addressed by the manorial courts – a special and peculiar

The 1839 tithe award map showing the farm of Lanacre and the river Barle. The fields between the manor and the river were known as court hams because the annual swainmote court was held there. There is more information about these local courts and the jurisdiction of the Royal Forest in Chapter 5.

In the 1839 Withypool tithe award schedule, field number 443, which is classified as 'arable', was titled Western Court Ham; field number 444, also 'arable', was titled Eastern Court Ham. The use of the word 'ham' is interesting because, although the original meaning was held to be 'enclosure', the usual meaning was of a flat, low-lying meadow by a stream. These two fields (unlike 445, 446 and 412) do not contact the river and are on ascending ground. Perhaps they were therefore more likely to remain dry and provided a more reliable meeting place to hold the courts. © South West Heritage Trust.

example being ours here, to be presently studied in greater detail.

In general these courts are better understood as gatherings in which agreements were made, rights asserted, duties confirmed and clarifications established rather than specific judgements made, as present day language might suggest. It could be claimed that, while petty justice was administered here, these constituted a form of democratic self-government where even the poorest could present a grievance and contribute to the discussion on policies regarding the common pasture.

The swainmote court was held at Landacre Bridge, where the fields were identified as *Court* Hams (1), and was attended by the free suitors who held tenements in Hawkridge and Withypool parishes and had common rights.

These courts may have originated from the three king's foresters who held Withypool and Hawkridge in Saxon times but the various duties and rights became formalised with the passing of time, as below (3).

The duties of the free suitors were:

1 To attend the swainmote courts held annually

2 To drive the forest on horseback nine times a year
    for horses, twice in winter and three times in summer
    for cattle, twice in summer
    for sheep, once for unshorn sheep

unclaimed animals being driven to the pound at Withypool

3 To perambulate the bounds of the forest once every seven years

4 To serve on the jury of the coroner's inquest on any dead body found in the forest.

The privileges of the free suitors were:

1 Common of pasture
      for sheep – one hundred and forty
      for horses – five
      for cattle – as many as could winter on the tenement
      for pigs – one sow, two pigs under two years old, one pig under three years old

2 Right to cut as much turf, heath and fern as they could consume

3 Right to fish in the rivers in the forest and precincts

4 Exemption from serving on juries, and to buy and sell free of all toll in fairs and markets.

The free suit tenements, for the most part in Withypool with a smaller number in Hawridge, usually each enjoyed one suit – for example, Halsgrove, Weatherslade, Foxtwichen and Garliscombe Mill. Some, like Higher, Middle and Lower Brightworthy, had one and a half. A few, such as Knighton, Higher Landacre and Lower Landacre had two, while Newland enjoyed three. These figures give an idea of the relative importance of the various farms.

The suitors at large from the other parishes bordering the Royal Forest also had to attend the court to retain their right of common. As time went on they sent representatives, having paid a fine for their own non-attendance. These became known as quit rents, and their documentation represents an important source of information as we shall show in the next chapter.

Their duties included maintaining the boundary with the entitlement to pasture their sheep, cattle and horses on Exmoor at half the normal rate. In time the declaration of this rate was to become known as 'crying the moor'.

With much of this concerning livestock we may ask – what animals would we see in medieval Withypool?

Cattle were of great importance as draught oxen, teams for those heavy wooden ploughs. There would have been large numbers of sheep – probably the native horned sheep of Exmoor – from which came wool, meat and dairy products. Goats provided milk and cheese. Hope Bourne raises the interesting suggestion that the semi-wild goats of Lynton may represent the descendants of these animals, creating another direct link with these past times.

One of the privileges of the free suitors was the right of free pasture for five mares and their foals. Horses were valuable not just as pack horses but as riding horses, and those feudal lords would have had their need for cavalry mounts. Although they are recorded as *equas silvestres* and *equas indomitas* (woodland and unbroken respectively) it is not clear how these categories correspond to their varying uses, nor where the native wild ponies fit in, although they must have been present and of value. The Exmoor Pony itself, such an essential and distinctive feature of the parish, will be more fully considered later.

We would also see pigs, the source of pork, bacon and lard, certainly in herds, for there are specific mentions of swineherds. But perhaps every reasonably successful peasant would have had at least a pig or two. They were probably much closer to what we would recognise as wild boar than our idea of a present day pig so one wonders how these individual animals were managed and herded.

Dogs must have been useful to control livestock and for general security, if not hunting. The forest laws included strict, even cruel, rules for 'expeditation' of potential hunting dogs to protect the king's hunting. This probably

Cattle on Bradymoor.
Photograph by Jo Minoprio.

only applied to mastiffs but it appears that only 'persons of worth' were allowed to keep dogs (4).

Domestic fowls and cats are two other groups which would have had useful roles to play, but the authorities had no desire to record their presence and we can only speculate.

At the crossing place down by the river animals drank and people gathered, and it must have been quite busy and noisy at times. Yet with so few inhabitants and the work that had to be done out on the common, in the woods and across the scattered small fields, our village – really little more than a hamlet – would have seemed to be a widely spaced and sparse settlement. Withypool would have been little more than a few farm buildings near the church with hovels huddled around. So perhaps absence and silence would be the overwhelming impression for a visitor from today.

Domesday usefully classified land into ploughland, pasture, meadow and woodland. While it is not specific about Withypool, we can imagine a relatively small amount of arable land but a fair amount of pasture in the sense of rough grazing, as in an outfield or even an area of enclosed moorland. Meadow was a better sort of grassland, such as the fields along the river, capable of hay production. There would have been more, denser woodland nearer the village than today, which was valued as a fuel source as well as building materials.

As the population surged during these centuries more of the wild land and tangled combes were colonised, new farms springing up through applications to the lord of the manor to take in the waste of some distant hill or make *assart* – a clearing – among the *silvae minutiae* – dwarf woodland or just scrub (3).

'Perambulation' was, literally, the process of walking round – a good way to check and find agreement upon what was to be included and excluded. Regular perambulations confirmed the boundaries of the forest, with its boundaries marking the beginnings of the various rights and responsibilities. Their documentations therefore represent a valuable source of historical record. This is particularly pertinent to the history of Withypool as it was on the edge and found itself at different times within and outside the forest. Similarly, Lanacre independently experienced its own changes.

The first perambulation was made in 1219 in the name of the young Henry III after King John was forced to disafforest all the lands unlawfully declared by him to be forest. As part of his land grab John had included Withypool.

In 1279 a new perambulation by 12 knights, foresters and verderers (a 'jury') established the bounds of the reduced Royal Forest but retained Withypool and Hawkridge, along with parts of Exford and Winsford.

However, this ended in disagreement so another perambulation took place later in the year. By following a line from Sherdon Hutch down the river to Lanacre, 'leaving that within the forest', then straight to Stonhuste (a stone that must have existed somewhere at the head of the little combe that has always marked the boundary of Lanacre on the east) and on to the Dermark (possibly the

Looking up to Sherdon. Photograph by Jo Minoprio.

small barrow in the middle of Bradymoor) it disafforested Withypool, except for the manor of Lanacre.

A third perambulation made in 1298 gives the same bounds but Lanacre was now excluded from the forest. As virtually everything else remained unaltered, we have to wonder what the special significance of Lanacre was and whether indeed its change of status was even responsible for the new perambulation.

Since the bounds at this point are still given as 'Deresmark' to 'Stonehiste', and so to the Barle, the only conclusion is that the boundary was diverted to run from Stonehiste across Bradymoor to Sherdon Hutch. Unless, of course, in the first place Stonehust or Stonehiste was not the head of the combe (the name would seem to indicate 'place of stones' and the scattered white stones to the west of Bradymoor at once spring to mind) but some place further west, and likewise the Deermark, a more westerly point (3). Perhaps the best we can conclude is that 'the relationship of Landacre to the forest has always been somewhat uncertain.' (4)

The 1298 perambulation gives a fine sense of Withypool with its 'woods, moors and appurtenances'. By this time the vast areas of waste had been divided up among the various manors as local common land (3). With its help – perhaps even imagining ourselves accompanying the motley group as it trudged round – we can imagine the patchwork of little fields, deep wooded valleys, a view of a small church, the nearby commons and the distant hills. A pattern of landscape had begun to be established which would determine the future shape of Withypool.

Further perambulations, as in 1300, serve only to suggest that a continuing unease or even tension persisted between the various stakeholders over the extent of the forest.

Objections to perambulations and complaints of their non-observance in the early part of the 14th century coincide with a general decay in the administration of the forest laws. The old idea of the forest was being gradually forgotten (3).

The catastrophic drop in the population at the end of the 14th century, when the Black Death stalked the country, and its consequent impact on the availability of labour and population shifts would have further contributed to these developments. But whatever the drift from the old forestal jurisdiction, alongside the complicated chops and changes of the entitlement to the forestership, our free suitors continued to maintain their traditional rights and activities. Thus, for example, we read that in 1470 Lord Dynham obtained a lease of Exmoor from Edward IV with 'the Courts of Swannimote' being specifically mentioned.

For now, however, it is enough to note this dynamic process of continuing change, reminding us that the Middle Ages were not a time of stasis and that inherent tensions between different groups evident even in Withypool – some of which we still face today, some 1,000 years on – and the methods developed for their resolution, can be traced back a very long way.

References

1   Mary Siraut, *Exmoor the Making of an English Upland*, 2009, Victoria County History, Phillimore, in association with the Institute of Historical Research at the University of London, 2009
2   Jeremy Holtom, *Exmoor Commons*, Exmoor Review, 2008, Vol. 49, p. 52
3   E T MacDermot, *The History of the Forest of Exmoor*, Barnicott & Pearce, The Wessex Press, 1911, p. 159
4   Hope Bourne, *A Little History of Exmoor*, J M Dent & Sons, 1968, p. 45

Chapter 5

The Manorial Courts of Withypool and the Manor at Lanacre

By Christopher Chanter

THE MANORIAL COURTS

The principle of a manorial court was that it regulated the availability of natural commodities within the land belonging to the manor. This could be water, grass, crops, fishing, turf, stone, gravel, mud, timber and any other resources that grew or lay within the boundary. Minerals also belonged to the manor.

There are very few manors with complete records of any length of time as there are at Lanacre in Withypool and, although they exist for only 60 years in the 18th and 19th centuries and for 10 years in the 20th, they are in remarkable condition and even include copies of some proceedings transcribed by hand. They give a unique insight into everyday life in a small parish and its inhabitants.

This study concentrates on the years 1772 to 1844 and from 1911 to 1921 when the last court was held.

Manorial courts would have begun almost as soon as a manor was established. Human nature being what it is, there is always someone who is either going to complain bitterly at the lot life has thrown at him or will try to get away with doing the bare minimum to receive the maximum. It was the court's job to provide fair regulation.

These courts were modest in their scope. They were more concerned with lists of rents received and due and monies owed than they were about punishing people. Any punishments were not for committing crimes but for taking liberties and not paying dues. They were never set up to try anyone for crimes against a person or property. So their purpose was never to compete with or replace the magistrates or assizes. They were only held every three years, which is infrequent compared to the Exmoor Forest swainmote courts, which were held twice a year and over the centuries sometimes more frequently.

The manorial courts and the swainmote courts had different functions. The swainmote courts were concerned with the goings on in the Royal Forest and the manorial courts were concerned with Withypool Common and whoever owned Lanacre at a particular time.

However, many of the same farmers had to attend both systems of court – the forest or swainmote court twice or even three times a year by the river below Lanacre, and the

1772

Rents payable to the Manner of Exton, and South Quarme, otherwise South Quarum, otherwise Withypool Sues, in the County of Somerset, to Mr. Jn. ...
Mrs. Babbedge, and Miss Wyott.

June the 2nd 1772.

Tenants	Owners and Occupiers	Years due Mich. last	Sum Total
Brightenworthy	Nash Pool Esqr. and his	1 — 0„3	0„3
three Tenements	undertenants Jnº. Trebble	2 — 0„3	0„6
—	and Henry Ley	2 — 0„2	0„4
Knighton Sd.	Mr. Pool Undertenant		
—	Peter Kingdon	2 — 0„4	0„8
South Batson	Mr. Geo: Stawell	2 — 0„2	0„4
Blackmoorland	Jnº. Hooper	2 — 0„2	0„4
Water Hous	Richard Howl	1 — 0„2	0„2
Woolpettland	Mr. Geo: Stawell	2 — 0„2	0„4
Uppington	Mr. Ven and Leders Tenants		
—	Wm. Titbal	2 — 0„2	0„4
Dadhay	Mr. Pool Tenant	2	0„4
Hillrody	Mr. Thos. Kent	1 — 6„0	6„0
	Henry Bullefent	2 — 0„2	0„4

October the 25th 1777, Recd. Do. to Michs. last of Mr. Stawell
May the 13. 1780, Recd. Mr. Geo: Stawell, to Michs. last

The oldest court record in the collection dates back to 1772.

The vellum cover of a book of manorial court records from 1821 to 1921.

manorial court every three years, held either at the inn or at the lord of the manor's house. This depended on where the lord lived, because for much of the time Lanacre was tenanted. Lanacre was, and still is, the manor house of Withypool even if the lord did not live there.

For example in 1257 the tenants who inhabited Lanacre were brought – or 'presented' – before the swainmote court for enclosing a piece of land in the Royal Forest – 'making a purpestre' – and were duly fined. However, they might have been quite within their right after 1298 to have done the same thing with the lord of the manor's permission on Withypool Common when Hawkridge and Withypool and Exton were taken out of the forest – or 'disafforested' – and were therefore not subject to its jurisdiction.

If they did the same after 1298 on Withypool Common without permission they would have been presented before the manorial court and fined. Regulating the forest and the adjoining parishes – its 'purlieus' – after 1298 gave everyone a space to settle down under a much less harsh regime and all went reasonably well until 1348 when the Black Death changed the system of agriculture.

Previously, the relatively labour-intensive job of growing crops, principally corn and beans, had mainly sustained the population. However, when the disease killed nearly half the population and decimated the labour force, there was a big increase in wages and therefore greater incentive to farm sheep and cattle. For example, it took a team of four to 'plough and sow and reap and mow', as the old song 'To be a Farmer's Boy' goes, but it only took one man to look after a flock of sheep.

The lord of the manor in most years did not personally preside over the manorial court even though the court may have been held at his house. The tenants represented the main source of his income and the last thing he wanted to do was to fall out with them. In general he left matters to his steward and bailiff. In addition there were 12 jurors drawn from the local people who were often tenants themselves, so any inquiry or proceedings were heard by the very people concerned with the matters before the courts.

Technically, attendance at this court was voluntary but anyone who did not appear – and many chose not to – would have to pay a fine. In the swainmote courts those who were summoned to appear for infringing the strict forest laws could be forcibly brought to the court – 'attached' – which meant that they were brought in with a man on either side grasping each arm.

The steward's job at the manorial court was to act like a parish council chairman to see the task in hand done and to see fair play. The lord of the manor simply pocketed the proceeds and, if the tenants were lucky, he gave them dinner.

The fines, such as they were, were mainly for not appearing when asked to do so. If you were a juror and did not turn up you were 'in mercy' and fined a shilling, which in today's money would be roughly equivalent to £50.

No-one from outside the parish would appear at the court leet – the name given to a manorial court – unless he was, for example, renting a piece of ground from the manor or had some business there. In a closed society in a remote location where the population was small it is difficult to see why anyone from more than a couple of miles away would want the trouble of tending to some business away from home. It was not like the Royal Forest where every year farmers would bring stock from up to 20 miles away to graze the moor. Through the process of 'crying the moor' grazing rights would be made available to anyone, as the price was advertised in all the local centres of population.

Withypool Common was grazed by adjacent farmers and the grazing rights went with the farms. Other commodities could be rented or bought by others but this was unusual. For example, if the manorial courts existed today and you drove a digger on to the common and excavated 10 tons of turf and sold it to the nearest garden centre you would not be brought before the manorial court. It would be a case of theft and a matter for the police and the magistrates. If they failed to take action,

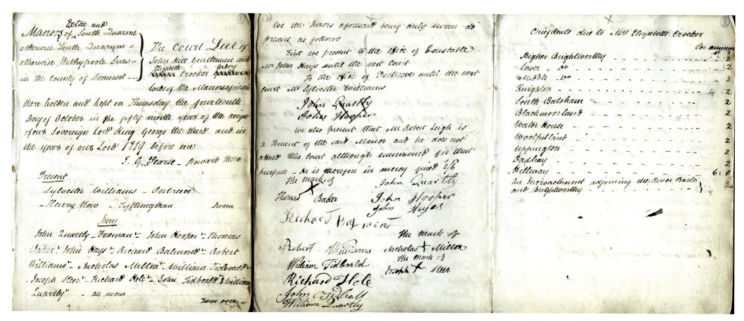

The complete court leet record of 1819, showing the entire proceedings.

then it would be for the county court in a small claims action for damages and restitution brought by the lord of the manor. The manorial court would not be involved at all.

In the days before the abolition of copyhold in 1922, if a stranger drove a pair of oxen and dug up the common, it would have been brought up before the manorial court, and they could report it to the police if they thought it was necessary. However, if you did the same before 1818 in the Royal Forest, you would be in big trouble and 'attached' at the next swainmote court – which after 1654 would be held at Simonsbath at James Boevey's house and not by the river below Lanacre – and be heavily fined. In medieval times that sort of 'encroachment' could mean slicing off an ear. So the difference between the two systems is great.

Before 1270 when the Justices in Eyre, who were the travelling senior judges and the highest court on Exmoor for the Royal Forest laws, met at Ilchester or Somerton, transgressors of those laws could be hanged or mutilated. However, the manorial court of Withypool never had the powers to do anything so drastic and was the centre of local life and eagerly awaited every three years.

The process of calling a court leet was as follows. About seven days before Michaelmas Day – September 29 being a quarter or rent day – the steward delivered a written notice to the bailiff to summon the tenants and persons concerned to make their appearance at the court leet – usually at the Royal Oak – on around October 14 every third year at 11am or 2pm.

After its inception in 1861 an advertisement would appear in the *West Somerset Free Press*. The notice was also posted on the doors of the inn, the church and the chapel. The court would be duly held and the accounts signed by the steward and bailiff and the jury. It is fascinating to see that in many cases between 1772, when the first record was made, and the mid-1800s the appearance of an 'x' to denote a signature by someone illiterate. This became less frequent until 1921 when, at the last court leet, there was just one 'x', made by a farm worker for the tenant of Lanacre who was one of eight children and was paid 50 shillings a year.

The only other officers to make appearances at the manorial courts are the occasional tythingman, portreeve and constable. The first two appear in 1811 and the last one in 1827. The tythingman goes back to the days of the Saxon hundred when that office made sure the king received his dues. The portreeve was like a mayor and, in a small place like Withypool, more like a spokesman for the people. The constable was a whipper-in to make sure everyone came to the court who was supposed to. These offices may have been revived in the 19th century for entertainment purposes more than anything – the prospect of a good dinner at the expense of the lord of the manor being a major incentive!

Let us now look at two 19th century manorial dinners.

In 1834 the court leet was held at John Hill's house at Newland; Mr Pearce was paid 16 shillings (16s) for attending as steward and 8 shillings and sixpence (8s 6d) was paid for ale and 7s 6d for beef.

In 1837 Mr Pearce was paid 15s 9d for attending as steward and the beef cost 12s 6d, dressing the dinner cost 2s 6d, bread and cheese 2s, potatoes and turnips 1s 6d, beer 6s 8d and grog 2s. Grog presumably was a strong ale laced with rum or brandy.

It is easy to see from the records how little the chief rents were. The chief rents were the rents payable to the lord of the manor for the privilege of being on his land and they amounted to just a few pennies a year.

The rack rents, however, were much more lucrative. These were for the commodities gleaned from the common; they were subject to demand and therefore

An extract from the court leet of Michaelmas 1827, which lists the farms and their chief rents and gives an idea of the relative value of each of the farms at that time.

much more liable to large increases. The chief rents were ingrained in time for so long that without inflationary pressures it was impossible to raise them.

For example, in 1772 Knighton Farm paid just 4d a year and owed 8d, in other words, two years rent. In 1831 Knighton paid 4d and owed 1s 4d, equivalent to four years rent. The rent did not change for 60 years. This was not rent for the farm itself but rent for the right to use the common. Like other farms, Knighton had been sold from the manor in 1700 under a private parliamentary act concerning Robert Siderfin's financial problems. In James Notley's first court leet in 1844 Knighton was still paying 4d in chief rent but only owed three year's rent so they were slowly catching up.

The records for rack rents start in 1798 when we find a famous hunting parson the Rev John Boyce paying three year's rent for a garden enclosed from the common. The amount was 7s, which was a considerable sum. William Tidboald paid 12s for three year's rent for a garden enclosed from the common. Mr Stear paid 1s 3d for cutting turf. Robert Horwood had three gardens at 2s 6d each a year and at the bottom of the page I was particularly delighted to see that wine 'half a galland (sic) for the perambulation' cost 10s, and quite right too!

The boundaries of most manors were perambulated or walked around once a year or less, providing the excuse for a convivial celebration. This was particularly important before enclosures, because the boundaries could be uncertain unless they were checked and everyone was happy.

A document dated 1842, giving the terms of cutting turf and using other resources from the moor for those without commoners' rights. The document shows the relative value of these resources: earth to make mortar at 2d for a 1,500lb load, sand at 4d for a 1,500lb load and stones at 6d a ton.

In 1844 the chief rent for George Cottey was a goose and 1s 6d. At this time the manor was owned by James Notley's son George, to whom it had been conveyed in 1843. A garden in the possession of Elizabeth Tidboald was now 3s a year. Cutting turf had gone up to 3s, more than double what it had been in 1798. Susan Tidboald built a house on the common and paid 2s a year. By 1847 Elizabeth Tidboald's garden cost 4s a year.

These rents remained the same until the records end in 1921 when the last court leet held. James Baker was portreeve, acting as hayward (with responsibility for maintaining the integrity of fencing and hedges), and was therefore in charge of the upkeep of the common. Tom Carter was bailiff, Ernest Chapman was steward, Harry Augustus Whittall was lord of the manor who had bought Lanacre from the Notley family and their successors.

The last court records of 1921.

The ubiquitous Tidboalds seem to have disappeared but there are Tudballs who paid 4s for their garden. Going back 100 years to when a garden rent was 4s, it was indeed a Tidboald who paid it, so we can only presume that the name Tidboald had become Tudball. There were Tidboalds farming at Culverhay, Wiveliscombe, until the recent millennium. On Withypool Common there are four fields called Tudball's Splats.

The manorial system at Withypool was succeeded by the Commoners' Association, which was formed in 1949 to regulate grazing on the common and the rights of those who were entitled to them. It would be wrong to say that the progress of that august body has been entirely smooth and without dispute. I am grateful to James Colvin whose father was chairman of the Commoners' Association for his quote from the *West Somerset Free Press* of November 11 1961:

'An article which had been published in a national Sunday newspaper about the Withypool Common grazing rights dispute caused bad feeling between the Commoners and the Lord of the Manor Mr Albert Huntley.

'"The expression of opinion that the common was overgrazed proved nothing," said Mr Huntley, "and figures were needed."

'"It was impossible to get the figures of cattle and sheep that had been grazed," said Major Colvin, "but it was obvious that the common had been overgrazed." He was backed up by Mr Milton who said that he had had to take off some stock. Mr Huntley said he had taken legal advice and could prove he was the legal owner of the land. No one had any right to touch anything on the common without his consent. Major Colvin said that "the Royal Commission on Common Lands report clearly stated that after the Lord of the Manor had exercised his rights in connection with his farm, he had no more rights until the rights of the commoners had been satisfied."

'He had discussed the matter with the commoners and they had decided to disband the Association and form a new one with a new set of rules. Mr Huntley refused to put to the meeting a proposal that it be disbanded claiming that it was out of order. It was finally decided that an AGM be called a fortnight later when new officers and committee would be elected and the rules would come under review.'

Definitely no dinner after that!

THE MANOR AT LANACRE

A manor means simply a piece of ground that has special privileges; it does not mean a grand house or large acreage.

Why then did Lanacre become the manor of Withypool and own a large acreage which over the centuries ranged between 1,600 and 2,000 acres? Manors belong to individuals or bodies such as the king, and those to whom he granted them, or sometimes churches and colleges. The important thing to remember is that the profits – or 'moiety' – go to the owner, and the owner of the manor could grant all sorts of commodities and sublet his privileges pertaining to the land to receive rents or payments for them.

Let us look at Lanacre's enviable position from the earliest times to answer its land holding question. The house and buildings stand halfway up a steep hill close to, but protected from, a track running to the south-west. The steading looks over the river Barle and has a commanding view. The point where the track crossed the river has always been important as it was used to bring goods from Devon into Somerset, which were two distinct counties and jurisdictions from the earliest Saxon times.

Watchet, Minehead and Bridgwater were all important ports and Dunster was an important administrative centre. I would like to advance the theory that the crossing place was not where the bridge is now but further downstream where the ford is shallow and the track can approach the road gently from the river. From the position of the bridge it would be impossible to scale the cliff up to the road level from the water, especially with a laden donkey, pony or mule, so the fording place would have had to have been across a shallow place.

There is a stone marked on an old map just above where I believe the track joins the present road. From Lanacre, therefore, the ford is visible whereas the bridge is not. So Lanacre is both strategic and defensive a place and, even if the manor was not there originally, but over on Bradymoor where ancient enclosures have been discovered, the view there of the ford is just as good, but is farther away from the track.

It was the Saxons who created parishes, hundreds and shires. The manors already existed in some form. A parish is a grouping of manors; a hundred was a way of garrisoning an area and deploying and paying the soldiers who protected the Saxon settlers; it meant a hundred warriors. Later it came to mean a hundred households. A shire was a large jurisdiction that more or less divided along areas of settlers: the Somersaetas; the Wiltonsaetas; the Dorsaetas. Devon and Cornwall remained largely Celtic and therefore outside the Saxon system of government.

Lanacre is on the border of two hundreds: the Carhampton hundred and the Williton and Free Manors hundred, both of which belonged to the king. Exford to the north is in the former and Withypool is in the latter.

The position of Lanacre meant that it was the last property in royal hands before the Devon border. It was also on the boundary of two hundreds, besides being an important fording place. With the vast Royal Forest to the west to keep an eye on, what more justification does one need for Lanacre to be not just a manor but *the* manor of the local area?

Lanacre was therefore a royal property next to another royal property – the Royal Forest – and their activities were intertwined even though they were independent of each other legally.

There is another manor in the area called Withypool Ivens, and an 'Ivaux' family are mentioned in ancient records but not in the Lanacre records. This second manor comprised land in and around the village, near the church and the community. There is no direct road from Lanacre to Withypool; the way is thoroughly roundabout. Could it be that the Saxon settlers in the 8th century left the village alone and set up their settlement further up river at Lanacre for strategic purposes and had nothing to do with the community, hence the lack of a direct way from one manor to another?

The manor in a village is usually in the centre by the church. So, although Withypool church was a chapel of ease to Hawkridge, it is an early foundation and it is quite possible that a church existed there when the invaders arrived. These invaders were not all Christian despite the fact that King Ine built churches and abbeys.

The defined area of the manor of Lanacre is easy to explain. The Royal Forest – which was, again, a Saxon institution – is to the west, the Carhampton hundred and Exford parish boundary to the north, the village to the east, and Devon to the south-west.

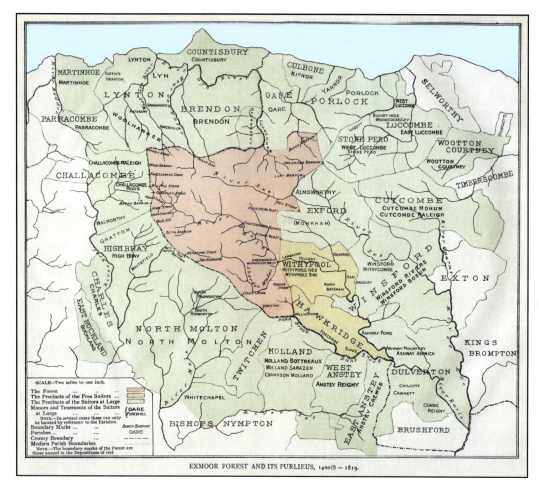

Exmoor Forest and its purlieus 1400 to 1819, showing the other manor, Withypool Ivens.

It was not until 1700 that the area over which Lanacre enjoyed manorial rights was considerably reduced. At that time a private act of parliament forced the lord of the manor of Hawkridge and Withypool Robert Siderfin to sell Brightworthy, Knighton, South Batsham, Blackmoreland, Waterhouse, Woolpitland, Uppington and Dadhay to John Houndle of Hillway, Withypool, by order of William Blackford master in chancery at Dunster. The sale included all manorial rights and customs, privileges, royalties, jurisdictions, commodities, advantages, profits, franchises and freedom from all courts of the said manors. This was because Robert Siderfin was in deep financial trouble.

Now comes the vexed question of why the manor of Withypool also extends into Exton parish in that it includes South Quarme, which is a farm in the parish of Exton in the Exe Valley.

After the Norman Conquest William the Conqueror appointed William de Mohun to be the first sheriff and he was given the manors of Cutcombe and Minehead.

Lanacre House, October
by Sir Alfred James Munnings.
Private collection.
Photograph by Chris Chapman.

The king, however, held the manors of Carhampton, Williton, Dulverton, Winsford and Nettlecombe as well as the Royal Forest which had been defined by King Alfred previously. At that time the forest also included Hawkridge and Withypool.

Subsequently, in 1199 the wardenship – or 'forestership' – passed to William de Wrotham who was personally given the manors of Hawkridge and Withypool. He also acquired the South Quarme manor of Exton. There was also a manor of North Quarme belonging to the Monceaux family, hence the origin of the local places Mounsey Castle and Mounsey Hill Gate.

It was William de Wrotham who divided Lanacre into two tenancies, Higher and Lower Landacre, and kept South Quarme under his own management rather than tenanted. It was during his time that the swainmote courts came into their own (1).

In 1402 there were three manors called Langmead, Ormonde and Barkley which seem to have incorporated much of the Exton and Withypool manor so some re-drawing of the boundaries must have taken place, which was quite common. In the records Langmead must be a misspelling of Lanacre because there is no other place to which it could refer. The Earl of Ormonde held land in Exton and so did Sir Maurice Berkeley, and the manor of Exton also included the manors of Hawkridge and Withypool.

It is important to understand that Exton was the dominant manor and the other two were subsidiary at the time. This is possibly due to the fact that Exton has better land. This arrangement of the three manors would have only been temporary and would have been leasehold from the king.

Modern Lanacre starts with the unpleasant James

Boevey, who features later in this history and who bought the forest from the commonwealth in 1651. To the delight of many, Boevey went to prison in Holland – his native country – under some contentious litigation. While he was detained he handed control over the forest to his deputy warden John Hill of Withypool.

Hill's grandson, another John Hill, became lord of the manor which was, and is still called the manor of South Quarum, otherwise South Quarme, otherwise Withypool Suis in the county of Somerset. This is the title on the cover of the vellum court record book. Presumably, this was after the 1700 edict forcing Robert Siderfin to hand over many of the farms on the western side of the parish to John Houndle.

It was at this time that the important manorial records began. All manors held courts before the abolition of copyhold in 1922 when the old manorial system of local government was swept away. Many still hold court leets, the occasional gathering of the manorial officials, for example in Watchet and Taunton, even though they are merely ceremonial and an excuse to have a convivial dinner!

In 1772 the court was held at the Hare and Hounds inn kept by Mr Adams in Withypool.

When the grandson of Boevey's deputy warden John Hill held court it was at his home Newlands. Lanacre was tenanted. Then in 1819 another historic shift affected Exmoor as a whole with the sale of the Royal Forest by the crown after 1,000 years.

John Knight bought the king's allotment and then acquired much of the rest of the old forest. The manor of Hawkridge went to the Acland family, and John Hill and Stephen Crocker, acting for his grandmother Mrs Crocker, were lords of the manor of Withypool Suis, which had long before absorbed the other historic manor of Withypool Ivens.

In 1843 the title and land passed to James Thomas Benedictus Notley of Combe Sydenham, Monksilver, who completely rebuilt Lanacre, allowing Higher Landacre to fall down while making a new Lower Landacre. There is no court record from that time until 1911 when Harry Augustus Whittall became lord of the manor.

After 1922 these courts were abolished but the manor does still exist as a legal entity centred on Lanacre and the grazing rights are still in existence. The age-old principle of 'levancy' and 'couchancy' still applies to the number of stock allowed, and the age-old occasional dispute over stocking quotas still rears its head as it did hundreds of years ago.

Today the Withypool Commoners' Association, which succeeded the manorial system in Withypool and now regulates grazing rights, is more or less harmonious, although the potentially controversial issue of overgrazing recurs.

The current lord of the manor is Jo Down who took over Lanacre through a transfer in the family from her stepfather Peter Hudson, who bought the property in 1977 and who died in 2011. She lives there with her husband Ashley and their son Louis, who will in time be the next lord of the manor of South Quarum, otherwise South Quarme, otherwise Withypoole Suis in the county of Somerset.

References

1 The Rev J F Chanter, *The Swainmote Courts of Exmoor*, Devonshire Association, 1907.

Chapter 6

Later Medieval Times

Many aspects of village life remained constant as the centuries passed. At the heart of the village is the church, which represents the best example of such continuity and something to which even today the visitor is powerfully drawn.

The church of St Andrew, Withypool, 'grey and weatherbeaten, with a low square tower'. Photograph by Chris Chapman.

The church of St Andrew, 'grey and weatherbeaten, with a low square tower' (1) is said to have originated as a chapel of ease to Hawkridge (2). A chapel of ease is another church building in the parish where worshippers can attend, if their parish church is inconveniently distant.

The Norman font in the church of St Andrew is evidence that the church enjoyed baptismal rights from at least the 12th century so must always have been the primary place of worship for our community. Photograph by Chris Chapman.

Normal services may take place there but there are certain restrictions. The ecclesiastical relationship with Hawkridge is discussed in more detail in Chapter 12.

However, with its Norman font – not the sort of item to have been easily moved – Withypool's church enjoyed baptismal rights from at least the 12th century, so must always have been the primary place of worship for our community.

Although much of the present building dates from the end of the 19th century, when considerable restoration took place, the fabric is impregnated by the history of the village. These stones, this special place sanctified by some 1,000 years of the markings of births and deaths, marriages and thanksgivings, prayers and lamentations, could tell such a story, were we able to hear it. We shall consider the church in greater detail later.

Perhaps contrary to first impressions the substantial bridge is not medieval but dates from modern times. However, here the river would have been crossed, at least when not too high, by a ford. Perhaps there were stepping stones, similar to the 24 rough-hewn stones half a mile downstream.

It is possible that there was an earlier bridge, probably made of wood.

There was a mill, which is likely to have been on or near the site of the present building. In the later middle ages some sort of hostelry would have existed to serve the needs of travellers, fewer of course at this time when travel was so much more difficult.

What is more certain is that we would see a variety of dwellings huddled round the church, ranging from recognisable cottages to hovels. There would have been all sorts of simple structures to protect and enclose stock, little fenced growing areas – vegetable plots rather than gardens – with muddy or dusty paths and lanes fanning outwards.

Withypool Bridge. Contrary to first impressions, the bridge is not medieval but dates from modern times. Photograph by Chris Chapman.

The main throughway passed somewhat to the west of the village centre at Lanacre. It is uncertain when the first bridge was built but it would have been important to take the main route across the moor from Dunster to North and South Molton over the river. We may imagine the strings of pack horses with their various attendants, people and other animals, plodding steadily in each direction.

Through the middle ages, then, our village pursued its life and traditions with its various peculiar customs, rights and duties in place and – for the most part – respected.

The old parchment rolls of the pleas of the forest record, among other things, the occasional imposition of fines for transgressions, such as poaching the king's deer.

With its swainmote courts and pound, in which animals caught unlawfully straying in the forest were impounded, Withypool could claim to be an administrative centre for the forest until the later part of the 17th century, when the newly built house and farm at Simonsbath became the headquarters of the forester.

References

1. Hope Bourne, *A Village of the Moor*, Exmoor Review, 1966, No. 7, p. 46
2. Guide to the church of St Andrew

Stepping stones across the river Barle below South Hill Farm. Photograph by Victoria Thomas.

Chapter 7

Towards Modern Times

By the 16th century rural England's population was increasing and we may assume a little village like ours would have reflected that rise. The south-west, which had traditionally been the last to experience change, be it invasion or technical development, now found itself in the foreground as the new world beckoned. Even its more remote hill country regions must have been affected by this sense of progress and adventure.

Certainly many farm buildings were rebuilt, extended and improved at this time of rising prosperity. The new farmhouse of Elizabethan times represents the traditional model of many an established Exmoor farm. Lower Blackland, for example, dates from this time: 'a pleasant dwelling, cream-washed and slate-roofed, with the bulge of the bread-oven marking the great hearth within' (1).

At the end of the 16th century some 40,000 sheep were put on to the moor in the spring until shearing time when they were driven down and 'told' – that is, counted. Any that remained were gathered in the pound by the bridge on the south bank at Withypool. Cattle, some 1,000 all told, would go out to the forest from May until October and there were about 400 horses which might stay either for the summer or all year round, depending on payment.

Unclaimed cattle and horses were kept in the field beside the pound for a year and a day, after which they were forfeit as strays (2). This forfeiture also applied to pigs, geese and goats as well, according to the deposition of John Court of Withypool (3). This gives us an idea of the mixture of stock that would have been encountered in and around the village. When Peter Hill of Withypool died in 1626 his farm produce comprised butter, cheese, hay, corn, geese and livestock. His sheep accounted for over a quarter of his wealth (4).

By the mid 17th century a great variety of documentations become available. So, for example, we may encounter in the Protestation Returns and Lay Subsidy Rolls of 1641 a list of names, many of which are familiar – John Hill, Christopher Webber and several with the surname Williams. Similarly, in the hearth tax exemption certificates of 1647, when those who were 'freed from the duty of chimley money because they have no visible estate that we know of . . .' more familiar Withypool names are listed. One wonders if they were as indigent as they claimed or was this a case of successful tax avoidance?

Painting of Lower Blackland by Hope Bourne who described the farm as 'a pleasant dwelling, cream-washed and slate-roofed, with the bulge of the bread-oven marking the great hearth within . . .' Doris Sloley Collection.

The parish registers which became available from 1653 represent an invaluable documentary resource as well, for example, show how families moved from one farm to another as sons grew up, married and took over tenancies that became vacant. Also listed is the number of baptisms where the mother is described as unmarried.

THE CIVIL WAR

Whether Withypool experienced any of the commotions of the civil war is uncertain but when a group of cavaliers passed through Exford in 1642 it must have been noticed, as would a large body of parliamentary cavalry withdrawing from Barnstaple when they crossed Exmoor on their way to Taunton in 1644.

Even more likely to have caused an impact would have been the cavalcade of 1645 when the future Charles II, then aged 15, set off in a fine company over Exmoor from Dunster Castle for Barnstaple. This well-established road wound its way from Exford to Simonsbath and then via Kensford Cross and Brayford to Barnstaple.

After parliament's victory, a new survey was undertaken in 1651 with the intention of selling these crown lands. This broadly confirmed the previous boundaries of the last perambulation, describing the use of the forest – or 'chase' – as 'very sound sheep pasture'.

James Boevey from London bought the forest, established himself at Simonsbath and set about making the most of his new acquisition. This involved demanding tithes from the pasturage of the surrounding commons, one of which was Withypool. Inevitably there followed litigation. Several of his most vigorous opponents, defenders of their long-standing privileges, were Withypool men. Thomas Pearse had gone round with the free suitors on his father's behalf in 1652 and twice since. He knew exactly where the boundary lay.

The various depositions are well documented (5) and give a useful insight into rights enjoyed, agricultural practices, numbers of stock and occupations. As before, the surnames are interesting in their continuity.

Thus 'John Hyll of Withepoole, Gentleman, aged 50', used to give public notice of the rates in the market towns. 'He has a right on the Forest for 420 sheep, 15 mares and foals, and as many bullocks as he can keep on his tenement called Newland in Withepoole . . . He has also liberty to take fearne, heath and turf and to fish, fowle and hunt . . .' (5).

The deposition of 'George Gulley of Withepoole, Husbandman, about 60', as pound keeper for 18 years, describes clearly the impounding procedure. He also tells how several areas of the common have been recently – and others more 'anciently' – tilled. 'It is an annual custom for the commoners of Withepool nine days before midsummer to drive the said common, and if any unshorn sheep are found, they are impounded and their wool taken . . .'

'Deliberate and careful, speaking of what they knew . . . these countrymen . . . built up an impregnable case against the testy little Dutchman' (6), a natural bully who was accustomed to prevailing. He lost, and from then on spent far less time in his fine new house at Simonsbath.

With the Restoration and Boevey's defeat Exmoor and Withypool regained its relatively quiet pastoral continuity, as we can gather from various quarrels that invoked the law, such as the Siderfin case of 1707 when even the forester himself regarded it as little more than 'a great sheep pasture' (5).

This picture persists through the 18th century. Many an Exmoor history now expounds upon the far-ranging

Exmoor Horn grazing above New House, Withypool. Photograph by Chris Chapman.

Sir Thomas Acland's Hounds by Hope Bourne, from *A Little History of Exmoor*.

hunts under the leadership of such as Sir Thomas Dyke Acland, who is relevant to our history of Withypool in that the diary of its sporting parson John Boyce tells us much about social life and activities at this time. These hunts, of more than 500 horses and '1,000 foot', must have involved many strata of society in and around his parish of Withypool.

The famous description of the village in 1792 in Collinson (7) may reflect the romanticism of the time but it justifies quoting as a thumbnail sketch – 'its situation is full of the wildest scenery: the hills are very lofty; some of them cultivated, and others heath or waste land, covered with fern and wild thyme, with many whortleberry plants and curious mosses.

'A track winds beautifully along the slope of these heights, overlooking the recesses of the dell, which is divided into fine pastures. Here no carts nor waggons are ever used, the roads being impassable for wheel carriages, and scarcely pervious for horses.' He adds that there were 30 houses and 170 inhabitants.

A picture of farming at the end of the 18th century can be gained from Billingsley's *Agriculture of the County* of *Somerset* (8). He describes hedges of beech as 6 or 7ft high and 4 to 5ft wide at the top but, apart from some of Boevey's enclosures at Simonsbath, the whole area would have presented a huge expanse of moorland with the occasional hill farm. These were being further improved, such as the house at Lanacre. Billingsley saw the opportunity for development, noting that water was plentiful and considering the land suitable for flax. He also remarked that although there was hardly a tree or bush to be seen, oak, firs, beech and elm would thrive.

There is much interesting information to be gained about prices and practices from his survey. Small horned Exmoor hoggits were bought at South Molton market on April 12 at about 10 to 14 shillings each, to be kept on the moor for two or three years for their fleeces, seldom exceeding 4lbs, which were bought at a uniform price at the farmers' houses.

Oxen – 'large, well made and almost red' – were yoked at three years old and worked for five or six years when they were sold to the graziers for £10 to £20 each. Meanwhile men earned 1 shilling a day and beer; women half that (sixpence) – with no mention of any beer for them. Meat (best beef, mutton, veal and lamb) cost 4d per pound; a turkey 3s 6d (three and a half days' work), goose 3s, ducks 2s 6d, and a couple of fowls 2s.

We are left with the conclusion that ordinary working people rarely enjoyed such luxuries, and that animals of every sort were very valuable.

But despite the optimistic suggestions of Billingsley and general improvements in agricultural techniques such as better crop rotations, this was still a rough and undeveloped landscape. There were no roads and no wheeled vehicles. Everything was carried by pack horse and the bridges, such as that at Withypool, were made for that purpose. They were narrow with parapets low enough not to interfere with their hanging loads.

Snell describes the old piers and abutments still existing in 1907: the line of the old North Molton track skirted the hillside, avoiding the wet ground to turn abruptly to the old bridge.

'The old, narrow village street which led down to the bridge has been mostly pulled down' he added (3). As it was not until the 19th century that the first roads to and from Withypool were built our description of these developments must wait for the next chapter.

By the end of the 18th century many ancient local courts had decayed and our swainmote court had probably degenerated into an assembly for collection of moneys, some formal recordings and, perhaps the most important business, the enjoyment of hospitality (5).

Although the new pound had been established at Simonsbath, Withypool was still being used in the 18th century – alluded to as the 'Little Pound' – when, for example, in 1736 the gate and wall had to be repaired, costing 1 shilling and 5 shillings respectively.

It was the hunting Sir Thomas Acland who was the last to be granted the lease of Exmoor. For £510 he extended his lease from the crown until 1814. But with the specific requirements of both the Royal Navy in particular and the demands of the Napoleonic wars in general, parliament was especially insistent on the use of crown lands as well as the need to grow forests for timber.

Instead of renewing the lease as a matter of course, the commissioners of his majesty's woods, forests and land revenues ordered a survey during which Acland renewed his application. The survey of 1814, which gives a detailed description of Exmoor including the rights and responsibilities of the Withypool suitors, led to the suggestion that 'an Act be procured for the Division and Inclosure' of the forest. The act received the Royal Assent on July 4 1815.

Misty up to Sherdon. Photograph by Jo Minoprio.

Landacre Bridge. Photograph by Chris Chapman.

References

1. Hope Bourne, *Two Exmoor Farms*, Exmoor Review, 1967, Vol. 8, pp. 74-77
2. Hope Bourne, *A Little History of Exmoor*, J M Dent & Sons, 1968, p. 76
3. F J Snell, *A Book of Exmoor*, Methuen & Co, 1903, p. 45
4. Mary Siraut, *Exmoor the Making of an English Upland*, 2009, Victoria County History, Phillimore, in association with the Institute of Historical Research at the University of London, p. 76
5. E T MacDermot, *The History of Exmoor*, The Wessex Press, 1911
6. Hazel Eardley-Wilmot, *Yesterday's Exmoor*, Exmoor Books, 1990
7. John Collinson, *The History and Antiquities of the County of Somerset*, 1791, reprinted 1983, Alan Sutton
8. John Billingsley, *General View of the Agriculture of the County of Somerset*, R Crutwell, 1795, p. 263

Chapter 8

The Nineteenth Century

THE SALE OF THE ROYAL FOREST

At the beginning of the 19th century, like many other moorland villages, Withypool would still have retained much of its medieval character. Thatched cottages would have been huddled round three centres – ford or bridge, water mill, and church – with muddy tracks suitable only for foot or pack horse traffic leading away up on to the surrounding moor.

Tracks also followed rivers and an old bridle path ran from Withypool up the Barle Valley and over Winstitchen to Simonsbath.

There was another one over Ferny Ball and Wintershead to Kensford Water, and so up Hangley Cleave to Two Barrows and on towards Brayford.

But the arrival of enclosures, the sale of the forest, the development of proper roads, population expansion and new agricultural practices changed this traditional picture radically.

ENCLOSURES

The practice of enclosing small portions of the commons to grow corn, mainly rye, had continued through the middle ages, but these were only temporary and after two or three crops had been raised they were abandoned. Many traces are evident around Withypool.

The process of consolidating the scattered strips in the open fields into compact holdings had been carried out over several centuries, especially in the more central areas of England. This enabled the occupier to hedge or fence in order to protect his holding from other people's stock, and then experiment with rotation of crops or to switch from arable to pasture.

Enclosures therefore encouraged innovation and more productive agricultural methods at a time of great growth

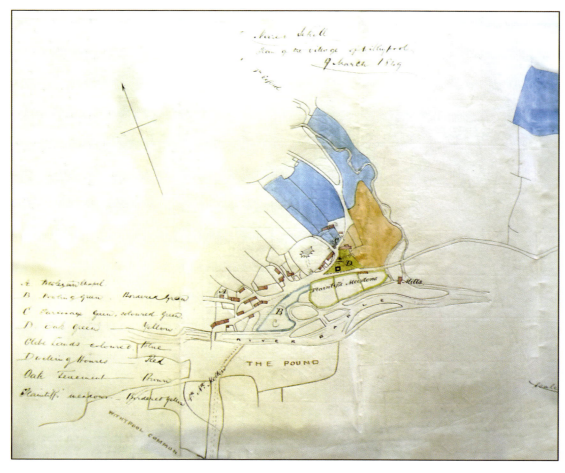

A map of Withypool drawn in 1849, showing the animal pound on the south side of the river.
© South West Heritage Trust.

in the population, but they were often unpopular as they led to the eviction of tenants and the depopulation of the countryside.

But for areas like Exmoor with their traditional, appropriate and acceptable arrangements, formal enclosure was not a controversial issue at least until the beginning of the 19th century. For Exmoor remained essentially unfenced from end to end, the different areas being delineated only by boundstones and landmarks.

But now change was in the air with inclosure awards which would represent the legal recognition of the radical change about to transform England's landscape. For Exmoor Forest these start with the award of October 20 1817, running through to the final of May 12 1819, with a sequence of awards in various parishes from 1848 to 1872.

Put simply, William the Conqueror's Royal Forest added up to about 38,000 acres. In 1819, out of the 20,122 acres of what was then the forest, about half was allotted to the crown (10,262 acres), 3,201 to Sir Thomas Acland, 1,633 to the free suitors (giving them an average of 31 acres each) and 4,700 acres to the suitors at large

(352 tenements in various parishes). John Knight bought the king's allotment with Simonsbath Farm and began his ambitious projects, but these developments did not directly affect Withypool.

Partly in response to this, in the 1860s a movement to preserve commons gathered momentum and as a result a House of Commons committee was set up in 1869. This coincided with a proposal to inclose Withypool Common which 'especially excited the ire of the committee' (1). Some negotiation followed but with the conclusion that no public advantage was to be expected, happily no inclosure took place.

As a result no inclosure of a common in the neighbourhood has been sanctioned since 1860 so Withypool – along with a few other commons – remains open (1).

THE TITHE AWARD

A detailed survey of the parish was drawn up in 1839 for the commutation of tithes ('confirmed by the Tithe Commissioners for England and Wales') with scrupulous measurement and identification of fields, lands and plots. This 'Apportionment of the Rentcharge in lieu of Tithes' represents an invaluable document with the details it offers of the situation, the purpose to which the particular area was given and names of owners and occupiers.

So, for example, at Lower Landacre, owned by George Crocker and occupied by Nicholas Milton, field number 415 called Over Ball Stitching was used as arable with a precise area of two acres, three roods and 10 perches.

Many of these fascinating names – Bake Splatt, Mutton Pie Meadow, Starve Acre – are not only descriptive, but entertaining.

The whole exercise gives us an accurate picture of the village in 1839 as we can be sure that people had to be satisfied with the figures.

So of the 3,404 acres – not forgetting the one rood and four perches – in the parish 1,297 were given to arable, 163 to pasture, 62 woodland, 1,850 commons, with two gardens and the glebe (belonging to the rector) accounting for 30. In lieu of tithes the Rev George Jekyll was awarded £165.

ROADS AND WAYS

Roads on and across Exmoor were notorious, as John Collinson mentioned in 1792. Indeed, some were so tenuous that they would hardly justify the title even of 'way'. Perhaps they followed broadly – and they would often have been broad, with foot and horse traffic swinging ever wider to avoid the central morasses – the courses of the ways seen on the first Ordnance Survey map. But even an expected way such as that from Withypool by Porchester Post and Willingford Water to Cuzzicombe Post never actually existed.

On the other hand, some ways which followed ancient field or natural boundaries, like Kitridge Lane, would have been more focused. In such cases, the lane being very narrow, a different set of problems could arise.

This was one of the last areas in the country to take to the wheeled carriage. Before that virtually everything was transported by pack horse with their 'crooks' – 'which are the receptacles of their goods, either wood, furze, or lime, or coal or corn, or hay or straw, or what else they convey from place to place: and I cannot see how two such horses can pass each other' wrote Celia Fiennes in 1698.

The largest of the Exmoor pack horses could carry a load as heavy as 400lbs with a distinctive long stride. Legend had it that they were bred from a thoroughbred, from a Spanish man-of-war wrecked at the time of the Armada, with a small, nimble native horse, which had to be an Exmoor.

'On they came without bridles or conductors, with their burdens brushing both sides of the deep cut lane. There was nothing to be done except to turn and fly to a wider place until the string had passed on, led by some veteran charger who knew perfectly well where he was going,' wrote Mr Vancouver in 1808, reminiscent of a contemporary meeting in one of our lanes with a large agricultural vehicle.

For the most part it was not until the 1830s that roads such as that from Withypool to Chibbet Post were properly surfaced. Even at that time there was no metal (a proper prepared stone surface) on the road to Dulverton. Archibald Hamilton, writing in 1907, gives us an idea of just how primitive transport and travel was:

'The first cart owned in Withypool was built . . . to the order of Mr. John Quartly, grandfather of the present John and James, who farmed at Weatherslade. The cart was brought over in triumph on a Saturday, but nearly stuck in the narrow lane from Exford – the only made road – as it was not wide enough. Next day the whole population went to church, and men who would resent being called old can remember being led there by their mothers to look at the great man who had brought the cart. He stayed several days to harness and break the horse. Mr. Webber, of Withypool, was carrier to Tiverton, and clearly remembers the road over Winsford Hill being metalled; from Comer's Gate to the head of Marsh Hill there was nothing but a series of ruts out of which it was impossible to turn a loaded cart. This must have been awkward if two carts met, but, as Mr. Webber explained, 'You never did meet anything.'

ISOLATION

Roads and communications may have improved in the first half of the 19th century but Withypool remained relatively inaccessible longer than many other places. In the surveys of 1838 and 1842 this inaccessibility was noted with the depression of property values because of the difficulty of getting produce to market (4). Much was spent on lime but the crops were light and ripened six weeks later than elsewhere.

A sense of this rural isolation can be gained from the intermarriage between local families. One example is to be found with the family of Joseph Steer who took over the tenancy of New House and its nine acres in 1797. His daughter Mary married Nicholas Milton of Lanacre and their grand daughter Elizabeth married Samuel Milton, living at Leys Farm (Foxtwitchen). Her sister married John Milton and lived at Withypool, while their brother John married Betsey, daughter of Samuel and Elizabeth Milton. Thus first cousins of first cousins on both sides of the family married.

The survival of this sense of isolation would have

contributed to a certain persistence of various deep-rooted superstitions even within living memory, so that as late as 1973 it could still be stated that 'Exmoor is a true pixie land' (5). Belief in them may have been widespread across Exmoor but Withypool seems to have been particularly rich in pixie lore.

One well-told story ran that the king of the pixies ruled at Knighton Farm but that with the pixies' dislike of church bells and their recent renovation he asked the farmer for the loan of his pack horses to take his wife and family 'away from the noise of the ding-dongs'. He obliged. Next morning the horses found their way home safely.

Another story tells how pixies came to Withypool farms to thresh the corn at night. Curious womenfolk at one farm peeped through a hole in the barn door and saw that they were naked, so put out clothes they made for them. The pixies took this as in insult and never came again.

In 1953 it could still be said that if you ask circumspectly and go gently you will find, especially among the older people, a surprising amount of lore about 'wicked women' and their powers (6).

Sally Pippin of Withypool lived in a little cottage higher up Pennycombe, or a barn later called Sally's Barn, now pulled down, on scraps of food, earning a few pennies from gathering bits of wool she bundled up. She was reputed to be a great hand at 'drawing a circle' (an activity inseparable from a witch's potency) and was said to have bewitched several people including one unfortunate man who lost all his hair as a result.

A more serious story tells how when she asked for some wool from a farmer, who dismissed her, a score of his sheep were found dead the next morning. Various bits of her story are still told. The rough cleave to the northeast of Higher Blackland is still sometimes called 'Sally's'.

Later practitioners included one Betty Rundle, remembered by a witness who was still scared of her long after her death. The story goes that when, as a girl, she was staying on her uncle Frederick Butcher's farm, every calf but one fell ill and died. Her uncle went to consult a 'conjuror' in Exeter who startled him by knowing what had happened and told him to treat well the person who came into his yard carrying a bundle of sticks.

Betty then appeared with her sticks and was duly and unexpectedly offered the milk she requested. Afterwards Mrs Butcher said to her niece 'Do you take the tongs and pick up that cup and take it out into the open. Put a big stone on it and leave it there. Not for the world would I let anyone else touch it' (6).

Among the other Betty Rundle stories is that of the 'urts (whortleberries) which the teller's husband resolved one day to have no more of from Betty. At which point Betty appeared, and cursed. Subsequently the trap turned over and the entire load was lost. 'Mr Clarke said he knowed he was witched . . .'

Another tells of Fred coming across a crock full of 'hundreds of toads big one and little ones'. And there is the story of the horse Tommy – well known in the Withypool district – which, when its owner Joe Donne refused to lend to Betty, was the cause of a 'wish' from her which almost killed Joe.

Meynell reflects that the power of 'wishing' survived well into the 20th century, along with many other minatory beliefs, such as those relevant to bringing snowdrops into the house, the importance of not moving rooted parsley and the value of a 'bung of fuz' (gorse) up the chimney to keep witches away.

A more positive result of this comparative cultural isolation was the local survival of folk songs. The distinguished musicologist Cecil Sharp working with the Rev Etherington discovered, transcribed and collected many folk songs, finding Withypool to be a rich source. The 68 year-old Joe Milton sang 'Still Growing' for him and Richard Thorne gave him the carol 'Come all you worthy people that dwells (sic) upon this land'. Ada Baker for her part sang another carol he recorded which some years later she denied all knowledge of. From Betsy Holland came the song 'The Murder of Macdonald', later to be published in *Folk Songs from Somerset* with a note about its setting in the rarely encountered Lydian mode.

EXPANSION

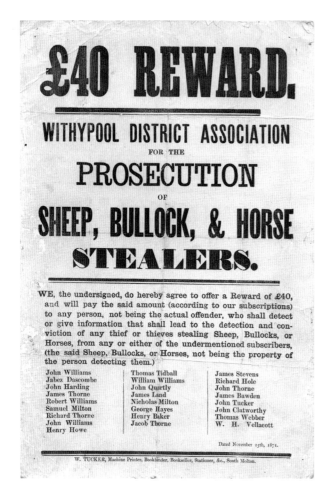

A £40 reward poster dated 1871.
Edna Clatworthy Collection.

As the century proceeded, southern Exmoor saw a big increase in the population which grew, for example, from 3,444 in 1811 to 4,752 in 1841 (4). With new techniques and machinery and the amalgamation of farms, much more of the land at Withypool became arable. There was less work for many, and for their part the more ambitious were ready to seek their fortune.

It was in 1861 that the village achieved its greatest population, dropping after that. The main reason for this was that, along with many other villages, Withypool exported people to the growing cities, London and beyond.

There may not have been the huge swings in population witnessed by the mining communities of North Molton or Molland, for example, but we read that in 1881 two Withypool men were neighbours in Swansea and two Withypool families lived on the same street in Camberwell, with a particular concentration in Mynyddislwyn, Monmouthshire (4).

In 1791 there were 170 inhabitants of Withypool in some 30 houses (3). In 1821 the population was 204, rising to 251 in 1841 and then to its greatest in 1861 when it reached 307. After that it dropped to 259 in 1871, to 197 in 1891 and to 146 in 1901.

Despite – or perhaps because of – increasing prosperity for some as the 19th century progressed there was serious hardship for others, especially the poorer labouring people.

The vestry meeting minutes give details of help to various people. For example, on November 9 1849 Ann Bryant's children were taken into the care of the parish, William being 14 and Mary Ann two years-old, both of whom were to die in the Union House. Further payments to this unfortunate family continue over the following years through Mr Quartley (then churchwarden) of Batsham (sic) and Richard Hole ('Guardian of the Poor') of Knighton. And at the meeting on April 24 1851 the vestry meeting decided to take a pauper, Mary Gully, 'to avoid law'.

The poor rate was quite substantial with (for example) Brightworthy paying £6 a year, Newland £4 and Garliscombe Mill £1.

With families of 10 or more crammed into a cottage, there was every incentive for the more enterprising to leave to find better paid work. Agricultural work was poorly paid and mining – dangerous and possibly involving farther travel – even worse.

It must come as no surprise that those left behind sometimes helped themselves in the only way they could see. The law was distant and certain valuable goods temptingly near to hand.

Steal the sheep and burn the wool
Goes the bells of Withypool

It was said that everyone was in it, robbing each other but united against the law. When a policeman was sent from Dulverton 'the wild men of Withypool' flung him into the river and stoned him, and would accept nobody but the parish constable whom they themselves elected (7). Perhaps all this helps explain the earnest wish expressed by John Hill in his will of 1862 that his children followed Methodism diligently so that 'they may acquire vital Godliness and to the utmost of their power promote and encourage the same in their houses and families and amongst their neighbours.'

Attempts at reviving mining in Withypool were made below Blackland near the Pennycombe river from 1875 to 1881 and in 1895. The adits had tramways and an incline to a loading bay near the road from where the ore went to Chibbet Post and so to Porlock, Minehead or Watchet Harbour and thence to South Wales.

The story of these mining endeavours follows a familiar pattern of mineral extraction on and around Exmoor – even when the ore offered useful potential, transport costs eroded the profits. Nearby Wheal Eliza, some of whose miners came from Withypool, is a typical example with its many stops and starts. The mine was re-opened and refitted in 1860 but work stopped there after just a few months.

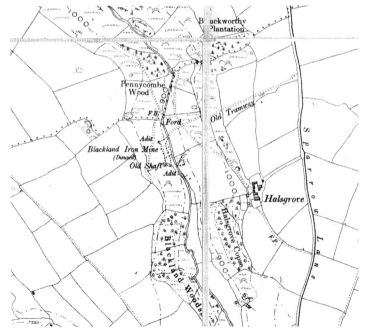

An Ordnance Survey Second Series map showing Blackland Iron Mine in 1902.

'It was never really a successful mine. This was due more to the lack of cheap fast transport away from the moor, than to the quantity and quality of the ore. This, as history has shown, has been the undoing of all the mining enterprises upon Exmoor during the past 100 years or more' (2).

Interestingly, though, there were to be further attempts at mining in Withypool, as we shall see.

The combination of serious poverty and mining bring to mind the infamous story of the unfortunate William Burgess who moved to a cottage behind the Royal Oak with his two children after his wife died. Depressed and convinced they would starve, he decided to kill them. The boy escaped but he strangled Hannah. After her body was found hidden in the Wheal Eliza mine shaft, Burgess was tracked down in South Wales, identified by William Reed, convicted and hanged publicly at Taunton.

The Withypool of the 1860s was described in *Kelly's Directory* as a village 'famed for its little horned sheep, and North Devon cattle', with 'four harvests a year – the turf, whortleberry, hay and corn.' Its inhabitants included Thomas Tidball, the publican at the Royal Oak, who also worked as tailor, and Thomas Webber at New House, who not only farmed, specifically dealing in butter and poultry, but was a carrier to Tiverton. It was he who remembered the road over Winsford Hill being metalled. Letters came by foot post through Exford from Minehead on Mondays, Wednesdays and Saturdays.

Methodism arrived early in Withypool, with some of the first meetings being held in 1809 at Hillway, the house of Joan Kenyon. Three years later a chapel was built by John Hill of Newland whose small burial ground remains, preserved as a garden (8).

A new chapel on a fresh site between the church and the river opened in 1881.

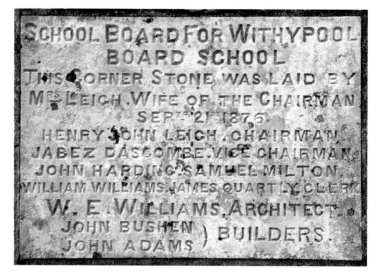

The School Board foundation stone laid in 1876. Photograph by Chris Chapman.

Over the following years the village continued to develop.

In 1875 a school board of five members was set up, with the board school (public elementary school) built in 1876 at a cost of £970 to hold (sic) 70 children under the mastership of Thomas Cook. The old school house (Wadmans) was built with stone from the quarry at Portford Bridge. Interestingly, the average attendance was recorded to be 42 – whether this reflected travel difficulties, the need to have children working at home, illnesses or other constraints is unclear. Certainly, average attendance was a statistic recorded over the years, usually running at about half the total number on the roll. In 1889 the mistress was Miss Katherine Barron, succeeded by Miss Mary Jane Ellis in 1894.

At the same time communications were improving. By 1883 the village had its own sub-postmaster Abraham Tudball, with letters arriving daily from Minehead at

11.25am and despatched at 1.25pm. One of several carriers, John Court offered regular services on Tuesdays, Thursdays and Saturdays and we encounter the first evidence of Withypool's future main trade in *Kelly's Directory* in 1889. Thomas Tudball advertises 'between Dulverton and Lynton and near the moors; facilities for fishing and good accommodation for visitors and tourists.'

By 1894 Abraham Tudball had diversified into the same business, announcing his 'boarding house, good accommodation for anglers and tourists at moderate tariffs; good stabling.' By the turn of the century Three Weirs had 'Boarding House' painted prominently on its side.

Nonetheless the village continued to seem self-enclosed and inward – or even backward – looking. Or was this beginning to be one of the reasons for visiting a Withypool that was learning to project a certain degree of quaintness – what might now be described as 'retro'?

A certain John Lloyd Warden Page, exploring Exmoor in 1890, visited Withypool and asked a man if there was anything to be seen, to receive the answer 'Nothing but a foolish woman, sir, who will be sure to see you' (9). He also mentions another incident quoted by Fortescue when the hounds chased the deer down the street while the recording barrister was holding his court and was left addressing no-one as everyone had rushed out to see the pursuit.

Superstition still persisted strongly, with a seventh son 'touching for the King's Evil', which would only work if both patient and toucher were fasting and if no charges were levied (5). And when in 1888 the search was on for the missing farmer who committed suicide in Pinkworthy Pond, a loaf of bread was launched on the water before the pond was drained in the belief that it would come to a standstill over the spot where he lay.

But with the arrival of new roads, better communications, increasing numbers of visitors, not to mention a greater self-awareness, Withypool was ready to enter the 20th century.

References

1. E T MacDermot, *The History of Exmoor*, The Wessex Press, 1911
2. J M Slader, *Days of Renown The Story of Mining on Exmoor and the Border Parishes*, West Country Handbook, No. 6, West Country Publications
3. John Collinson, *The History and Antiquities of the County of Somerset*, 1791, reprinted 1983, Alan Sutton
4. Mary Siraut, *Exmoor the Making of an English Upland*, 2009, Victoria County History, Phillimore, in association with the Institute of Historical Research at the University of London
5. Jack Hurley, *Legends of Exmoor*, The Exmoor Press, 1973
6. Laurence Meynell, *Exmoor*, Robert Hale, 1953
7. Hazel Eardley-Wilmot, *Yesterday's Exmoor*, Exmoor Books, 1990
8. Noel Allen, *The Churches and Chapels of Exmoor*, Exmoor Society, 1974, Microstudy F1
9. John Lloyd, Warden Page, *Exploration of Exmoor*, Seeley and Co, 1890 – limited to 250 copies

Chapter 9

The First Half of the Twentieth Century

LIFE IN WITHYPOOL

We are given a fine description of life in Withypool – population 146 in 1901 – at the beginning of the 20th century by F J Snell when, as he puts it, he stumbled on Blackmore's track in 1900:

'Mr. Tudball, the village postmaster, whose father was landlord of the Royal Oak for 27 years, can vouch for the fact that Blackmore wrote part of Lorna Doone whilst staying at the inn. On one occasion the novelist and his wife strolled down to the bank of the stream, where Mrs. Blackmore sat down under the shade of a tree. A pretty incident ensued. As the children of Mr. Land, of King's Farm, tripped along on their way to a hayfield, she stopped them and chatted pleasantly with them. By-and-by Mr. Land himself appeared, to whom she smilingly apologised.

"I am afraid I have hindered the children."

"No matter, ma'am,' replied the farmer: 'their work isn't very valuable."

Mrs. Tudball, having prior to her marriage been a dressmaker in the village, made Blackmore some shirts, and, after the visitors had left, Mr. Tudball received from them a welcome present of strawberry plants.'

Snell describes how he, like Blackmore before him, happily chatted with villagers, keen to pick up scraps of information, which he equally happily embroidered, merrily confusing fact and fiction (1).

More factual, however, were the reminiscences of Walter Raymond, an established and famous author, who lived here for a dozen years from 1905, writing essays for various periodicals such as *The Spectator*. He was celebrated locally as Somerset's Thomas Hardy and accompanied Cecil Sharp on his wanderings around Withypool as he collected folk songs, introducing him to the gypsies who were camping on the common. Rev Francis Etherington (the senior) also helped Sharp.

'His cottage, with its "half hatch" opening on to the village street, was a meeting place for all and sundry . . . as an exponent of rural life, he will always be remembered by those who, as he himself, value the products of the mind and character of the rural people of a past day; "those who perceive the preciousness of simple things"' (2).

View of Withypool showing the church without its tower c 1900. Edna Hayes Collection.

One shilling (5p) a week was the rent for his cottage, with its old beams, half door, chimney seats and bread oven. It was cleaned for him daily by a zealous Mrs Critchell, who supplied him with eggs costing 1s for 16 and chickens at 4s 6d (22.5p) a pair. At the village inn he drank in a kitchen furnished with oak settle and rush-bottomed chairs. The landlady came in from her dairy to serve him, for most publicans were farmers too. Raymond described his drinking companions affectionately, the labourers and skilled craftsmen (2).

The thatcher with his bat, hazel spars and wheaten reed piled high on the yellow wagon was one such. It would have been made by the village wheel-wright, superb master of a difficult craft, whose name Noah Pike was emblazoned in red upon the tailboard. The frames and spokes of his cart were oak, sides and felloes of elm, floor of deal, the hanging-pillar of ash and he made the tires (iron rims) in his own forge, possibly fired by old tailboards and felloes.

Such a wagon was driven by the carter, whose fore-horse bore brass bells, crimson tassels and a protective crescent moon in brass polished to the lustre of gold.

Spars of hazel or withy for the thatcher, along with poles and sticks for all sorts of jobs, came from the hedger or woodman, who also supplied the hurdler.

Humbler occupations included the tranter, who carried goods and packages to and from local towns like Dulverton or Wiveliscombe, the hawker selling his small domestic items, the strapper (itinerant hired labourer), the mole catcher and the snail catcher, whose captures went to Bristol glass blowers because they were 'good for the chest'.

As ever, of course, there were the farmers. Although some still cut corn with the sickle, the sheaves hand bound by a few of the older women, there were now machines 'drawn by a team of great sweating horses' that did both jobs.

In 1901 we can learn from a bill paid by Mr A Huxtable, the huntsman, to Fred ('Granfer') Reed who worked for him, that a cow cost £11, a heifer £7.10s, a pig £10, a yearling £3.15s, a ram £2, and a ewe 3s. The man's wages were £1.10s.

'After harvest came Thanksgiving with a gargantuan tea that included jam of Exmoor whortleberries, Exmoor honey, clotted cream, and afterwards the company danced traditional dances, "Hunt the Squirrel" and "Wave the Handkerchief", and sang old songs like "The trees they do grow high and the leaves they do grow green".'

Similar descriptions of the impact and celebration of the changing seasons and their festivals come from Edith Macdonald when she arrived in 1907 to take up the post of headmistress of Withypool school, which she held for 32 years. After three years Edith married the farmer who lived next to the school.

Those happy days were recollected by their daughter (3), when in winter farmers rode to the school, carrying

The Royal Oak in the early 1900s.
Rita Westcott Collection.

baskets filled with hot dinners for their youngsters. School finished early to make sure the children got home in daylight. A favourite pastime was throwing snowballs through the open kitchen windows along the way – many a ball landed in the frying pan. There were parties and concerts at Christmas, with gifts off the tree.

Every year a rich neighbour presented each child with a book and a large iced bun with a cherry on top – the cherries were inclined often to disappear beforehand; the bun (without the book) was forthcoming at Easter too. Whitsun meant singing in the chapel, now gone, while the summer brought outings with the parents to Bristol Zoo or the seaside – though there was a dreadful tragedy on a later occasion which we shall hear about. During the first world war school ended early so that the children could go and pick 'urts (whortleberries), which fetched high prices and were used for dye – the proceeds provided clothing for the children.

Although this glimpse of those early years of the 20th century before the First World War may seem sentimental, these are contemporary descriptions. Life must have been blighted by hardships, many a loss and much untold suffering, but for sure there were happy occasions, a great variety of celebrations through the year and with the passing of the seasons a sense of fulfilment to compensate.

An example of boisterous fun was the Exmoor custom of 'drowin' o'cloam' (throwing the crockery) on Collop Monday. Described by Elworthy in 1875, it was still going strong in Withypool in the 1920s, according to the Rev R A Newman, rector from 1919 to 1932 (4).

On the night before Shrove Tuesday, if the outer door was left unfastened, it was quietly opened and a sackful of broken crockery thrown indoors, the perpetrator escaping (if he could) before being observed. When dumping the crocks, or alternatively throwing dirt or stones at the door, the intruder repeated a doggerel, asking for a pancake.

'Any young men in the house would then rush out and try to seize the miscreant. If successful, they blackened his face with soot and gave him a pancake. It was said that it reminded the household that there was a need

An invoice paid by Mr A Huxtable to huntsman Fred ('Granfer') Reed in 1901.

Bessie Blackmore feeding the hens outside Fair View in the 1930s. Barbara Adams Collection.

to be shriven the next day, but it sounds as much like an opportunity to have some good-natured rough and tumble.

Another more formal annual event was the summer races, sports and gymkhana. They were held in the middle of August on the racecourse at Comer's Gate. A programme from those early years (1923) describes the various events, beginning with a race of 'about one mile' for ponies up to 12.2 hands. This was followed by the All Comers' Challenge Cup race 'of about three miles' and the Farmers' and Tradesmen's (same distance). There was also a variety of athletic races including the Smoking Race (foot) – I would like to be able to give you more details – and finishing with musical chairs, in which one brave woman – Miss F French from London – competed against five men. Unfortunately, I can find no record of whether this was a mounted event nor who won the prize cup when the prizes were awarded at 7.15pm.

Although, as mentioned, competitors came from far and wide, there was many a local name such as Rawle, Burnell, Williams, Westcott and Clatworthy. And after all these strenuous challenges, the evening was rounded off with a public dance held at 9pm in the school room, with admission costing 2 shillings, which included refreshments.

This fixture waxed and waned over the years, but

was revived with enthusiasm in the 1940s, raising funds for the Minehead and West Somerset Hospital and the Soldiers', Sailors' and Airmen's Families' Association, typically attended by some 600 people. An extensive report on the 1945 annual races in the *West Somerset Free Press* described Withypool's sporting fixture as 'one of the most popular events . . . as far as Exmoor and the districts adjoining it are concerned.'

A favourite item had been the Turf St Leger when spectators enjoyed 'the sight of half-a-dozen cart-horses pounding up the half-mile straight to the finishing post'. In 1945 this gave place to 'a parade of cart-horses, of which four appeared in harness.' There were relay races, the Moorland Scurry (for children not over 12) and the Exmoor Derby, during which Miss M P Harris, daughter of Air Chief Marshal Sir Arthur Harris, chief of RAF Bomber Command, who was staying nearby, was thrown. Corpl Cyril Meadows of the Withypool section of the St John Ambulance assisted:

'Happily she pitched clear of other runners. She was brought back to the start, where she was given attention for concussion, and after recovering somewhat she was taken home by car.'

Among the many other events were Stopping the Tufters (for children not over 16), Express Letter Race, Ladies' Messenger Race, the Walk, Trot and Gallop, Potato Picking, Bareback, Open, a Mile Cycle and a Mile Foot Race. This last attracted 'about a dozen entries (the highest in the horse races had been 14), and most of them finished.'

'There was no lack of the sporting zest which characterises Withypool races and produces 'hell-for-leather' gallops that fill the spectator with a sense of satisfaction and give this fixture its distinctive reputation.'

Nor did the fun stop there for, as before, there followed a dance attended by about 170 people, which went on until 1am 'when the National Anthem brought another annual event to a close.' (*West Somerset Free Press*, August 25 1945).

One activity that brought virtually everyone out was hunting.

There were the famous Devon and Somerset Staghounds, reinstituted by Mr Bisset in 1855 which, while covering a huge swathe of country from the Taw to the Parret, from the Bristol Channel to Tiverton, often hunted over our area. On September 14 1899 one great hunt saw a run from Hawkridge to Glenthorne.

An example of a good hunting day and the turnout can be found in *Country Life*, November 30 1935:

'Just before eleven o'clock Ernest Bawden comes up the hill from Lanacre with the bitch pack... a hard-driving lot, fit to run for their lives. After a short consultation . . . hounds move off towards West Water, followed by a large field composed of local followers, visiting fox hunters from up-country, a good sprinkling of sporting farmers mounted on cobs or wiry native ponies, and about 200 cars . . .'

Two hundred cars in 1935 Withypool certainly attests to the huge popularity of hunting.

Along with stag and fox, there was hare hunting. Here is a typical page from an edition of *Harriers Journal* for a meet at Withypool on Monday October 16 1939 when, with 15 1/2 hounds on a 'sunny, very hot' day, the scent being 'very good' two hares were killed.

'Drew up moor towards Greystone Gate, hounds feathered on a line and a hare jumped up, ran around then crossed Worth Bottom left handed to Worth Brake back to moor where she was killed after a very pretty and fast hunt of 20 minutes. Anthony Norton and George Goodall got pads. Drew towards Fourfields found and ran to Halscombe Allotment swung right handed below

Withypool Hill then up to Greystone Gate and across to bog where she was killed. Very good hound work . . .'

Another hare was found but 'hounds were whipped off as we did not wish to kill a third hare'. All the attenders were then listed, with names including Mrs Aston, Walter Blackie, Mary Etherington, April Bridger, Capt Cox, Col Smith, Mrs Munnings, Miss Hope Nelson, Mr and Mrs Robinson, Mrs Hesling, Vera Lock, Ethel Blackmore, Hooper and friend, Fred Burnell, Tom Barrow . . . finishing with 'Bertha Clatworthy, Jim and Albert Delbridge, 2 Hawkins and 2 others.'

Another more selective but much enjoyed sport was shooting. A handwritten personal journal shows great variation from year to year in the numbers of grouse killed. In 1938-9 it was just three, with six blackgame ('a very wet cold summer'), but in the following year the figures were 22 and one. By 1963 Capt Gibbs commented that there was very little game 'and the shooting is privately owned.'

Fishing has always been popular. For some, the likes of Fred Barrow, it was a case of a simple hook and line, but richer people such as Lord Russell came down from London and the home counties specifically for the pleasure of fly fishing. It was a day's car journey in 1929 when Lady Russell drove down on a Friday, returning – 'because of the election' – on Sunday, but coming back once more on the Tuesday. She enjoyed the services of a chauffeur. They must have put a high premium on their Withypool fishing to justify all that to-ing and fro-ing.

A taste of the enjoyment such people derived from Exmoor fishing can be found in *Fishing on Exmoor* (5) – 'my best basket . . . was sixty six . . . with an electroplated angel minnow.'

The Barle was full of fish in the early 20th century. In *The Autobiography of a Poacher* (6), a classic tale of a poacher turned water bailiff, the protagonist was employed by Sir Thomas Acland to net the pools between Sherdon Hutch and Bradley Ham, when 3cwt of fish was taken, which were distributed by Sir Thomas amongst his tenants. At Withypool Bridge the nets were so heavy they had to recruit extra help. With a trammel net at night he would catch 20 or 30lbs. He also tells how he caught a salmon poacher at Withypool who used a spear to catch his fish.

But important as hunting, shooting and fishing were in bringing people to Withypool, many others came simply to visit. For some, like the cyclists in those inter-war years, it was the travelling that was part of the pleasure. For them and for others – then as now – it was to enjoy the moor, the place Withypool and the warmth of the reception. They were all sorts of people: a few, as we have seen, decidedly aristocratic, some well-to-do, along with quite a few ordinary folk.

For many Withypool people, having paying guests became an increasingly important activity and source of income as the 20th century progressed. The Reeds at Bridge Cottage proved to be very popular hosts, with their visitor book attesting to a great variety of very satisfied visitors.

Col Green and his family from Tonbridge spent two very comfortable days at their 'dear little cottage', the Millingtons found kindness itself with no effort spared to make them comfortable in their fortnight and Mr and Mrs Sanders from Amersham gratefully recorded that 'even the baby slept well'.

L Richardson from Morden wrote 'stayed the night at Knighton. The trouble of loosing (sic) my way was amply compensated by the wonderful reception received. I hope to be back again soon.'

The Cyclists' Touring Club produced a large number of guests from all over the country, with two stalwarts arriving on their bicycles on Good Friday evening April

10 1936, having left London at four o'clock in the morning. All were hospitably catered for and nearly all returned, some again and again.

The Davies family from Leatherhead in Surrey came for a night in August 1939 and stayed for five, but we must remember that war was threatening.

'We are truly grateful to Mr. and Mrs. Reed for all they have done for us during our stay. We go away with very warm recollections of Withypool – the glorious moorland scenery and the beauty of the lush meadows along the Barle have made a deep impression, but deeper still perhaps is the impression of the warm hospitality and friendship of the people who live in this delectable spot. We have tramped over many miles of Exmoor but have yet to find a place that meets our conception of the ideal centre for a holiday, whether it be a strenuous walking holiday, or the more restful kind, which implies long hours in a deck chair in peaceful surroundings.'

No explanation or apology need be made for these lengthy quotes, for they speak for generations of visitors to Withypool and illustrate and explain the crucial role of visitors, tourists and holiday makers in the life of Withypool over the last 100 years.

From November to Lent there were all sorts of winter entertainments, with weekly whist drives in the church room, and rather grander ones in the village hall. On one occasion, for example, the Free Press reported a 14-hand drive with Fred Barrow as MC and the prizes, contributed by the WI, presented by Mrs Trezise. Mrs S Blackmore won first, Mrs B Williams second, with Mrs V Coward the consolation. For the gentlemen, first was Mr S Bowden, second Mr R Coward and (I can only quote from the Free Press) the consolation prize was won by Miss M Common.

The celebration of St Andrew's feast day, the great poultry whist drive in the week before Christmas (first prize a huge goose) and many another party livened up winter evenings, but particularly impressive were the plays and pantomimes.

'Cinderella' for example, written by the members of the drama group, featured a beautiful golden coach lit by fairy lights in which rode Cinderella (Anne Bowden). 'As each member entered, appropriate music was played, and by clever acting they revealed the role each was to play . . .' Many familiar names occur in the cast list, with Joyce Etherington the fairy queen, Harry Reed the demon king, Peggy and Eleanor Common the ugly sisters (May was busy behind the scenes), Tom Barrow the baron, Marion Ingram the baroness, Edna Barrow the prince, Winnie Bowden the page and Heather Bowden and Berta Robinson the fairy horses, with Arthur Ingram the coachman.

It must have been quite an evening as it included a sketch by the Young Farmers entitled 'A Scheme in Hyde Park'.

Another play in the WI hall was 'the mid-Victorian comedy, in three acts, by T W Robertson (1867) presented by the talented local company, produced and directed by the Rev. F M Etherington.' The cast list included Capt Wardrop, appropriately playing a captain, and Mr E M Heale along with members of the Bawden and Blackmore families.

'The players deserve every credit for the way in which they rounded off their characterisations with polish and smoothness,' commented the Free Press. Although it noted that the military uniforms were not quite in keeping with the period, it gave credit to Mr Etherington who acknowledged this in his introductory remarks, asking for the audience's forgiveness. 'Considering the limited facilities common to Withypool . . . and allowing for unavoidable minor faults, it was a thoroughly good show.'

WITHYPOOL IN THE SECOND WORLD WAR

Withypool played its part in the second world war not only by sending men but by contributing to the war effort in many other ways. This included offering hospitality to the supreme commander no less – as well as large numbers of American troops (described later) – and accepting evacuees.

Many came from very poor families and were infested with scabies – though some think it was the American troops who imported the mite. Either way, there was a certain separation of the children at times, with the evacuees being taught in the WI hall. However, there are happy stories of acceptance, inclusion and friendship as well.

Terry Hannan who came from Leytonstone to stay at Westwater was one such. Another was Margaret Hicks who came to Knighton in 1943 aged 11, from 32 Kingston Road, Leytonstone, London E11 – the then six year-old Millie Reed remembers the address even today. Many years later she went to see where her friend had come from, but found no trace of the house or street – everything was gone. Perhaps it was as well that Margaret had come to Withypool.

Stella Carroll recalls a happy stay at the Blackmore's farm (7). The little girl, who felt as though nobody wanted or cared about her, was warmly welcomed by Madge and Fred. She joined the village school, just a two-roomed building, with the easy-going and caring teacher Miss Condon.

'Withypool at that time seemed almost self-sufficient, with everyone growing vegetables and salad stuff. Bread, butter and milk were all home-produced, fruit too; even the lambs' tails were cooked . . . Sometimes we'd go down to the river Barle, paddle and catch small fish. In good weather we'd go up to the moor and pick 'worts'. There was no fear of traffic or strangers then, as we never saw any; the only form of transport was farmers' horses and carts . . .'

After four years she went back to London to find her family 'complete strangers'. Her mother found it hard to understand her Somerset accent. 'I told her once I didn't like her and I wanted to go home to Auntie Madge and Uncle Fred. I got a clip on the ear for that.' Some 48 years and five children later she returned to find the village which was as she remembered it.

Evacuee children with their visiting parents Mr and Mrs Tilly. Doris Sloley Collection.

'We stayed overnight at the Royal Oak and were given a very warm welcome; and when we went down to the river, I couldn't resist the urge to take off my shoes and paddle in the clear water. I felt like a little girl again.'

Another visitor to the Royal Oak was General Dwight Eisenhower in 1944, in command of the three million troops who made up the allied expeditionary forces, then scattered across southern England. 'I'm enjoying myself' he told the Dulverton stationmaster as he saddled up and rode across the moor, on his way to our village, to find – like many another traveller before and since – rest and refreshment. He spent the night at the Royal Oak where a copy of his signed photograph is proudly displayed behind the bar.

This photograph shows Eisenhower with his British chauffeuse Kay Summersby (with whom he is said to have had an affair) and the daughter of the then owner of the Royal Oak Mrs Smith, near Waterhouse Farm.

Years later, the time of secrecy long past, a West Somerset man Henry Kingsbury living in California forwarded an article in the *West Somerset Free Press* – 'the paper from home' – to the president. 'Thank you for mailing me the clipping,' replied Eisenhower. 'It brought back memories. I very much enjoyed my few days on Exmoor and I wish they had been more.'

Henry Williamson, of *Tarka the Otter* fame, also spent a short time in the village during the war. One night in 1940 this deeply disturbed and alienated man, like many other first world war soldiers, more damaged than was generally realised, being unable to sleep 'switched on the light and tried to read of another man's attempt to leave a part of the earth fairer than he found it.'

John Knight's ultimate failure at turning Exmoor into decent agricultural land, like that of his native Worcestershire, resonated with his dejected and despondent mood. The moor, he wrote, was

Portrait of General Dwight Eisenhower.
Barbara Adams Collection.

'unconquerable'; it was as constant – as 'ageless' – as mankind's propensity to violence. A week later he was in prison, arrested like his friend Oswald Mosley as a suspected Nazi sympathiser (8). The astonishing question arises as to whether his arrest might have been organised by another Withypool man of great influence, whom we encounter later on.

In many ways it was a time of hardship, with petrol

General Dwight Eisenhower riding with his chauffeuse Kay Summersby and Mrs Smith from the Royal Oak on Withypool Common.
Barbara Adams Collection.

and other commodities in short supply, but the Robinson family, like Stella, recall happy times. Going to the cinema at Minehead turned into quite an adventure – the children rode their ponies to Exford, where they were stabled at The Crown, then they caught the bus to Minehead. If there was time, they would play on the beach – in their riding clothes. Unfortunately, they had to miss the last quarter of an hour to catch the bus home, but the experience of the whole day made up for the truncated film.

Everyone had to walk then, or get out the pony and trap, so there was much more opportunity to talk, pass the time of day and generally keep in touch. Village social life was further enhanced, if not excited, by the Americans who were camping a little way down the river. The officers came up to houses such as Holmbush for much appreciated baths.

Margaret Hutchings (née Robinson) recalls riding out to watch their bombardment of Larkbarrow and Francis enjoyed the drama of a decidedly reckless American who tossed a hand grenade into the river to catch some fish. His father, a colonel from the first world war, spoke sternly to the commanding officer as a result.

In the absence of their parents, the Robinson children were nicely looked after by Miss Westcott. Food was plentiful. They remember how there were huge numbers of rabbits – Winsford Hill was perforated by burrows so care needed to be taken when riding there – which were an important source of meat, with many being sent up to London.

The children also helped with the house cows (which had to be walked to Winsford to the bull). In short, they enjoyed a wonderful outside life, walking, riding and fishing. In the evening they played cards with neighbours like the Goodalls at Three Weirs. Their dog was a loyal and energetic spaniel-terrier cross called Scamp. On one occasion their father drove them to church at Exford (the stern colonel was a Baptist, who preferred the low church there to the much higher church at Withypool) where they were surprised to be met by Scamp.

The appearance of the village changed and the houses that were originally painted white were often camouflaged – especially those that were prominent, and so might help guide enemy bombers on their way to Bristol and Cardiff. Margaret Hutchings remembers Holmbush turned green. In fact, many enemy bombs were dropped on Exmoor, even if they were being dumped by homebound raiders, with Lanacre and Winsford Hill identified as 'collecting' points (13). Two, presumably stray, bombs fell on Lanacre.

Another, totally different but equally captivated wartime resident was Sir Alfred Munnings, President of the Royal Academy. Withypool and the warmth of its people won its way deep into his heart too. It was Millie Reed who delivered an important telegram one morning (a good way for a child to earn a valuable two – old – pennies) to Mr Munnings. After that, it was *Sir* Alfred. A favourite day for him would begin with Pineapple, Ernest Bawden's ex-hunter, being brought to the door of his house next to the village church, with a gallop on to the common, some painting, and then back in the evening to family and a large number of assorted dogs (9).

Among the many stories of his painting in the village is the occasion when, spotting granfer Rawle crossing the river on his horse, he asked him to stop so that he could capture the picturesque moment. Granfer had better things to do than sit on his horse in the middle of the river to be painted, so replied politely, 'No time today sir, I'm

Lady Violet Munnings.

sorry'. The family of course now wish he had bothered to find the time.

The Robinsons remember Lady Violet Munnings well – a kindly person with a sense of humour, well disposed to children (fortunately, unlike her husband, not fond of swearing) and devoted to horses and dogs. 'Meeting Violet on Exmoor you were aware that she was always watching you. This trait made her fascinating to a child. She made you feel important. The wide set eyes, the smile, the rosy lipstick; you felt she was acutely aware of your thoughts, your mood, your interests. She was able to attune to the longings of other living creatures; it was the secret of her mastery over animals . . .' (10).

The daughter of a London riding master, she showed horses for her father from the age of 12, and won the gold cup at Olympia in 1911. She hunted with a Pekingese on the horse's withers, and another dog on a long lead. After the war Margaret Hutchings met her in the members' enclosure at Ascot. Lady Munnings called her over. 'You'll never guess what I've got here,' she whispered. And, pulling up her sleeve slightly, she revealed the

Sundown on Exmoor by Sir Alfred James Munnings. Private collection.
Photograph by Chris Chapman.

Pekingese. After his death, she had him stuffed and used to carry him around, even when hunting.

Sir Alfred opens the second volume of his autobiography with a lovely description of a letter accompanying a parcel of hugely appreciated butter from his old friend Mrs Bawden of Newland Farm (11). Reading the letter, he reminisces affectionately – 'I see the stone-built farm – the Red Devons – the sheep – the fowls – the Muscovy ducks. I hear her saying the words, 'Froude and I hoed all the swedes and mangolds and cabbages (five thousand) ourselves . . .'

Munnings painted some important works at his studio in Withypool, including a famous portrait commissioned by the king of the jockey Gordon Richards on the mare Sun Chariot. He depicted local views as well, including a fine view of Lanacre painted from Brightworthy, which appears in Chapter 5, and *Sundown on Exmoor*, reproduced here. And when in 1944 the Withypool races were revived Sir Alfred acted as one of the judges, providing extra prizes.

All was not play, although Withypool somehow succeeded in making even serious activities such as forming a home guard entertaining. The mixture of ages and denominations as described by one of its members (Gordon Williams in his *Exmoor Farming – The Way It Was*) sounded very like *Dad's Army*, with 'a Major Lieutenant as leader (a shopkeeper/post office proprietor), two Sergeants (a blacksmith and a carpenter), a Staff Sergeant (garage owner) and others, including one or two who always had something to sell to make a bob or two.'

This formidable fighting force included George Wensley, Fred and Jack Clatworthy, George Burnell, Cyril Meadows, Bob and Reg Williams, Wilfred Milton and Percy Harris. Meetings were always on Sunday mornings, but there were training visits to the Blackdown Hills and Dunkery and exercises against neighbouring village platoons. One such occurred at the Sportsman's Inn when, by the time our intrepid attackers finally reached their destination, the defenders had given up and gone home. However, a pint went down well in the inn. Another manoevre saw our platoon defending the bridge at Withypool.

Still, there was training with real weapons such as live .303 rounds, Molotov cocktails and hand grenades – a flavour of which emerges from this description by Gordon:

'The grenade used for practice had a seven second fuse. Having taken the pin out, Sid Ridd (nicknamed 'Pull Through' as he was apt often to get stuck and have to be pulled through), accidentally dropped it behind him instead of throwing it over the top. We heard a flurry of feet back around the corner before the explosion and no doubt Sid was ticked off but luckily no-one was hurt.'

Withypool Home Guard.
Doris Sloley Collection.

When the Americans arrived in large numbers serious training exercises took place regularly, with artillery gunnery practice nearly every day sending shells whining overhead from various points, including Withypool Hill, directed to a target area behind Larkbarrow House. Silence abruptly returned with the sudden departure of the thousands of American troops for D-Day. Many stores were left buried on the moor which were excavated by resourceful villagers and put to good use in those austere times. When the home guard was disbanded, all firearms and munitions were handed in, but members were allowed to keep their tunic, boots, badge and a great coat, which must have been appreciated in the vicious winter to come.

On May 11 1945 (Millie remembers the exact date as it was her baby brother's birthday, which is relevant to the story) the Americans who were about to depart offered the local children rides over Withypool in their tanks.

With the arrival of his new son, her father Fred refused to let her go, to Millie's chagrin. She adds that those tanks scarred the moor badly.

Another potentially serious threat to the landscape was the need to increase the home production of metal ores. The Home Ore Department visited Exmoor in 1941 when initial tests suggested useful prospects, especially at Blackland. Canadian sappers set about clearing a fall, but the lode was disappointing, soon running out and the ore not of the preferred quality (12), so once again mining in Withypool was abandoned.

There were some interesting, indeed remarkably appropriate Exmoor defence arrangements. A home defence force was created from the ranks of the Devon and Somerset Staghounds, after it had been suggested that horsed patrols offered the best means of covering large tracts of hill and moorland and that members of the local hunts would know every yard of ground.

'Thus, in a moment when the might of fully mechanised warfare was being demonstrated on the Continent, the enterprise of the Exmoor riding country restored the horse to wartime . . . The Exmoor Mounties, their background a famous hunt, claimed to rank as Britain's senior mounted guard' (13). They were inspected by no less than a former chief of the imperial general staff. One of their watch points was Brightworthy Barrows. On one occasion, to his patrol's misgiving, a recruit presented himself on a cart horse, which slowed things down, but the problem was resolved when he and his mount 'came to grief' (unspecified) in a ditch on Withypool Common, and they came no more (13).

On September 7 1945 the vestry meeting discussed the proposal of Capt Helmsley to raise a 'Welcome Home' fund for ex-service men and women whose houses were in the village and were not receiving a welcome home gift from any other parish. The hoped for £150 was exceeded and the presentations made, with sports for the children, on June 8 1946.

References

1. F J Snell, *A Book of Exmoor*, Methuen & Co, 1903
2. Evelyn Clark, *A Meeting with Walter Raymond, Poet*, Exmoor Review, 1966, p. 33-34
3. Vanessa McMullen, *Exmoor Review*, 1990, Vol. 31, p. 11
4. R W Patten, *Exmoor Custom and Song*, Microstudy G3, The Exmoor Press, 1974
5. Claude Fitz-roy, *Wade Exmoor Streams – Notes and Jottings with Practical Hints for Anglers*, 1903. Reprinted, (Kessinger Legacy Reprints)
6. '*Caractacus*'. *Autobiography of a Poacher*, edited by John Macqueen, 49 Rupert Street, London, 1901
7. S Carroll, *Wartime in Withypool*, Exmoor Review, 1995, Vol. 36, pp. 21-22
8. William Atkins, *The Moor*, Faber and Faber, 2014, p. 37
9. Estelle Holloway, *Sir Alfred Munnings at Withypool*, Exmoor Review, 1994, Vol. 35, pp. 48-51
10. Estelle Holloway, *Woodbine Cottage where the Bing boys lie*, Exmoor Review, 1986, Vol. 27, p. 59
11. Sir Alfred Munnings, *The Second Burst*, Museum Press, 1951
12. M H Jones, *Wartime Mining on Exmoor*, Exmoor Review, 1979, Vol. 20, p. 41
13. Jack Hurley, *Exmoor in Wartime 1939–1945*, The Exmoor Press, 1978, p. 77

Chapter 10

The Second Half of the Twentieth Century

These post war years may have been a time of austerity, but reading news items from the *West Somerset Free Press* one gains the impression that our village thrived, expanded and developed with a huge variety of activities involving the whole community. Before television and easy travel, small settlements had to make their own entertainment, which Withypool most certainly did.

THE VILLAGE EXHIBITION

The village exhibition, organised by the Rev Michael Etherington in 1949, is a good example of the activities that went on in the community. 'The richness of Withypool . . . in family treasures which have been handed down through the centuries was remarkably illustrated . . . in the Church Room . . . as a means of raising funds towards the cost of constructing a garden around the room . . .' announced the Free Press.

Mr A I Ingram (retired lawyer, chairman and clerk of the parish council and bit part actor in the drama group, to mention just a few of his roles) had prepared a number of documents relating the history of the village. China, pictures, needlework, toys, coins, and even the star of the Order of the Garter worn by King Charles on the morning of his execution, which he personally presented to Capt Basil Woodd as an acknowledgement of his loyalty were all on show.

Among other 'things of interest' that were gathered and presented was 'a most beautiful' 16th century violin, still – it was claimed – used on winter evenings to make music for the village to dance to, along with a flail 'used at Foxtwitchen about a century ago and still occasionally put into action', and a 15th century horseshoe.

The paper describes in detail a painting of a Jack Russell by Capt Charles St John Mildmay, which belonged to his sister Mrs Hamilton (her name perpetuated in the name of her house, as with many others in the village of Withypool). Rags was then 14 years old and 'the last of the genuine Parson Russell terriers' – referring to a recent controversial correspondence on Jack Russells – 'and he lived to reach the grand old age of 17.'

With all these exhibits 'the whole effect was that here was a community proud of its past, alive to its present, which, when it decided to put itself on show could do so in a most attractive and interesting way' (1). And we too may echo these comments: what other little village would

Evan Lock beside Hillside Cottage, leading his carthorse Royal down Sandy Road to feed the cattle. Mr Lock sold milk from his dairy at Fir Tree Farm in Withypool on his return from the war. Di Pershouse Collection.

or even could present such a wonderful exhibition, and who now would not love to have visited it?

THE VILLAGE HALL

It was in 1955 that the Women's Institute offered their hall, which had been built in 1928, to the village. Mrs Ingram, the chairman, explained that having spent heavily on the hall over the previous three years, the WI did not have sufficient funds to enlarge it, as had been asked of them.

Improvements were certainly required. Shirley Scoins and others recall a somewhat primitive hall in those WI days, very different from the excellent present structure. But as we have already heard, many were the dances, parties, shows and social events that the old hall had hosted over the preceding years so it had a good record of service. The place was known affectionately as 'the tute'

Withypool village hall and members of the Women's Institute. Tony Howard Collection.

for many years, even after its change of ownership and improvements.

However, Edna Clatworthy remembers her brother-in-law's wedding breakfast in the old hall, when the various items of food were prepared the night before and carefully laid out. Next morning, the family were horrified to discover that rats had destroyed the trifles . . .

An electricity supply was connected in 1955, with what sounds like a very jolly celebration attended by many – including representatives of the South Western Electricity Board (SWEB), one of whom appropriately presented the hall with an electric clock.

In 1961 ownership of the hall was finally transferred and in 1964–1965 funding from the Ministry of Education and Science, matched by local funds, paid for the new cloakrooms and kitchen.

Further appeals in 1966 to the Withypool community were very successful and an unexpected offer of a further grant from the ministry of £1,100 allowed the second stage of rebuilding to go ahead.

It must have felt as though all these successful efforts finally achieved proper recognition when the BBC's *Any Questions?* team broadcast from the newly rebuilt Withypool village hall on April 21 1967.

THE FETE AND FLOWER SHOW

Founded by Geoffrey Scoins, and now in its 60th year, the Withypool Fete and Flower Show has always been a popular event. Initially, it took place in King's field by the river, followed by a dance. More than a few of the names of the original committee members are still involved – the 1958 list including those of Barrow, Scoins, Coward, Reed, Clatworthy, Maclaren, Huxtable, Bawden, Sloley, Westcott and Williams.

There were 348 entries to the flower show in 1957, rising to more than 600 in the 1960s and they now run at an impressive 300 to 400. Profits from the flower show have risen from some £40 in 1956 to about £2,500 in 2013 and have enabled many improvements to be made to its venue, the village hall.

A typical report in the Free Press describes in detail various aspects of one fete and flower show when the prize for the tallest flower was awarded for a thistle measuring 7ft, and a wild flower arrangement which featured 86 varieties was exhibited. The fancy dress parade marched from the school through the village, escorted by a mounted troop, also in fancy dress, representing characters in Lorna Doone. Sports events included 70yd flat races, high and long jumps, three-legged, obstacle and sack races, along with egg-and-spoon, thread-needle and mixed pair races (for adults, mother and son and father and daughter).

Mr C Pearse of Langford Budville judging potatoes at Withypool flower show in 1991. Photograph by Chris Chapman.

TWO TRAGEDIES

But two tragedies struck Withypool in 1952: one involving the loss of two lives that affected the community, the other a community tragedy with no loss of life that affected many an individual.

A happy band left Withypool in a coach for a seaside trip one summer's morning, never for a moment expecting what the day would bring. On July 23 1952 the rector of Hawkridge and Withypool the Rev J R M Etherington (the junior) was drowned on this church outing while attempting to save the life of a boy, a server, caught in the tide at Instow.

Fifteen year-old Norman Huxtable, the rector and others were playing quoits on the beach when the tide was out at a spot called the Point where there are deep sandpits. 'It is believed the boy lunged forward to catch a quoit thrown by the Rector who was standing in deep water. Finding himself out of his depth, he clung to the Rector and both were dragged under' was one newspaper's account. Their bodies were not recovered at first, so the sad party returned to the village with two fewer people than they set out with.

The Rev Michael Etherington's funeral service on August 2 was described in great detail in the *West Somerset Free Press*. The bishop of Bath and Wells spoke movingly to the huge congregation which spilled out into the churchyard, with a large gathering of clergy from near and far. Clearly he was a much-loved man, as was demonstrated by this moving description:

'. . . the many floral remembrances which were laid on the turf on both sides of the pathway from the entrance gate to the church porch. Among them were numerous bunches of flowers gathered from cottagers' gardens, and simple tributes from children. In the church, on either side of the altar, was a mass of gladioli blooms and pot flowers, which had been arranged by Miss M L Todd, and the grave was lined with bracken fern, heather from the moor, and simple flowers gathered from gardens in the village . . .'

Among the many mourners were his parents, his father having been the previous rector, retiring only four years before in 1947. He, like his son, had been a much loved

In Memoriam

The Reverend J. R. Michael Etherington
M.A., B.Litt. (Oxon)
RECTOR OF HAWKRIDGE AND WITHYPOOLE

Born: Minehead, 15 March, 1913   Died: Instow, 23 July, 1952

Buried in St. Andrew's Churchyard, Withypoole

minister, involved in a wide range of parish and local activities from school management to performing and producing amateur dramatics, from parish council work, to – as we have heard – collecting folk songs. He also supported the Exmoor Horn sheep breeders' and Exmoor Pony societies.

The Free Press goes on to list the attenders, as was the custom, which gives us a useful list of Withypool residents at the time. The parish council recorded on behalf of everyone the great loss sustained by his death – 'His sincere devotion to the two churches and their congregations, as well as to all parishioners of the two villages and his generous and keen interest in all their activities were appreciated by all.'

Their simple wooden crosses in the churchyard with their crucifixes are deteriorating now, but this was the Etherington high church wish: that such monuments should have a limited life and, just as living memory fades, so should the memorial. This may pose a problem for those who retain loving memories of these good people and all that they did for the village, but happily the restored medieval cross near the porch stands as a permanent memorial.

After this Michael Etherington's father stood in once again as rector, from July to December, until the Rev Hopkinson took over. A learned man with a strong academic background, not perhaps the sort of rector one might expect to find in a little Exmoor parish, the Rev Hopkinson was a much-loved and diligent priest.

When John Land's family fell ill he attended promptly on horseback, as was his wont. Several tell how he would often visit and enjoy a cup of tea; he is still remembered with deep affection.

WITHYPOOL IN THE 1952 FLOOD

Floods were not that unusual for those who lived down by the river – people knew that the important things to do were to remove the bottom drawer (or two), pick up the rug and open the back door. There were of course no electrical plugs or fitted carpets, and the wooden chairs came to no harm. But this flood was different.

Hazel Eardley-Wilmot describes this catastrophe eloquently. On Friday August 15, strolling down to the ford at Knighton – 'along the northern horizon lay a horribly sinister cloud, without motion or shape; it was sheer indigo density to an immense height, merging at the far edges into dark grey. Awed, I thought what an atrocious storm somebody must be having . . .' (2). That evening, when 10 minutes before nothing was unusual, a flood of wild water flowed over the bridge, over the road, and into the lower cottages.

'It was already impossible to leave them – water was rushing past the doors. The elderly people inside pulled the bolts home and went upstairs to hope for the best.'

Millie Reed tells how they knew this time was different when they heard the sewing machine afloat, bumping around on the floor, and drowned sheep swept past the house.

'The old Bowdens, both over eighty, had gone up earlier. "Sam", said the missus now, "there's someone at door. You'll have to go down". He went half-way down, and found water up to the third stair; the door was not very firm, and he could not reach it. But if his legs were shaky with age, his head was not. Back he climbed – "Have 'ee got a mop upstairs, Mam?" She had, and he

The flooded garden at Riverside Cottages. Doris Sloley Collection.

went gingerly down again and propped the door with a mop and stick wedged against the stairs. He got rather wet, but no more water came in' (2).

By daylight the worst was over. Village and valley were a sad sight, desolate as a battlefield. The good old bridge still stood, but beyond it was a huge crater full of muddy water where grid gates and hedge-bank had been wrenched away. Walls, garages, cars and sheds were gone, gardens and their soil washed clean away, leaving a black crust like lava. Although some animals were lost, many survived. Margaret Hutchings remembers how their horses – two ponies and a hunter – found the highest point in the field and waited sensibly on their little island for rescue.

Communal spirit and good humour were quick to surface. Already daughter and grand-daughter were shovelling mud out of the Bowdens' cottage; the dairy man (a first world war veteran), whose three new ricks and milking shed had disappeared, chaffed them as he passed – 'I can't think how people can get in such a mess when there's so much water about!' Somebody hailed the river bailiff when he came down to the post office: 'Here's the man who's supposed to look after the river!' (2)

During the following week the tidying-up continued, with help from a Women's Institute party who came by bus equipped with scrubbing brushes and pails. The Red Cross brought food, clothing and carbolic and council workmen were busy on the torn road. Farmers found most of their missing animals, which had escaped uphill. One way and another, despite the loss of hay, the terrible damage to hedges, fences and gates, and the removal of a lot of earth, Withypool put itself back together again.

Here was proof, if proof be needed, that a community can help itself.

Two days after the flood Earl Fortescue, the lord lieutenant of Devon, and Lord Hylton, that of Somerset, launched a relief fund. It was thought that perhaps £200,000 might be raised, but the actual figure was nearly £1.5 million. The money was disbursed with a graceful personal letter, individually signed.

A pleasant and perhaps surprising postscript to the flood and the widespread positive response from everyone from far and near who rallied round, is the letter of congratulation that the parish council sent (proposed by Mrs Bidie and seconded by Mrs Reed) to Mr Bustamente of Jamaica when he was included in the Queen's birthday honours list. He was a minister who had been in England at the time of the flood, and had personally superintended the distribution of the free gifts of sugar and bananas from the people of Jamaica to the people in the flooded areas.

As one stands by the bridge today, looking out over the soft green river banks and pretty little gardens, it is difficult to imagine the devastation wreaked that 1952 night.

VILLAGE LIFE IN THE MID-TWENTIETH CENTURY

As we have heard, there was a rich social life in Withypool which included annual events such as the flower show and harvest festival, dances and other gatherings in the hall, weekly whist drives, conviviality at the pub and various hunt meets.

Often though it seems people were happy just to meet up, pass the time of day over the garden wall or lean over the wall of the bridge to chat while watching the fish (there must have been more then), and then go about their business. Certainly, life was simpler. Fred Barrow remembered no crime, or even mischief – although he did mention poaching – and there was no village policeman.

The Padmores, who lived at Mill Cleave, were the only people who owned a television set, so it was there that many villagers went to watch the Coronation, crowded around a little screen.

In fact, in that year after the flood, which had brought so much damage to the village, a variety of reconstruction and fresh developments began to appear. Some 32 mountain ash of six varieties, one copper beech, three lime, two rhododendrons and 100 common beech had been planted on land adjoining Riverside Cottages and the grid to celebrate the Coronation.

The annual parish meeting heard that 'The South-Western Electricity Board is contemplating bringing electricity to Withypool from Wheddon Cross, via Exford, and has sent forms to householders who might be supplied.'

And, importantly, building began on those much-needed new council houses.

'A good deal of road repairs and improvements have been carried out by the County Council, and the Parish Council thought that the parish had at last had its fair share of attention' – reading the parish council records certainly confirms that this grievance had been constantly aired. And this is not to mention that 'the County Council had also undertaken to erect name signs at the approaches to Withypool from Sandyway and Comers Cross.'

Derelict cottages below School Lane were demolished in 1955 and 1956 and in 1957 the parish council requested the education authority to have electricity connected to the school. It must have felt that Withypool was at last entering the modern world.

But life was changing in the wider world. Employment prospects in small rural settlements were decreasing, with many other villages apart from Withypool experiencing the emigration of the young, a relative increase in the older population and an overall drop in numbers. Inevitably the school roll dwindled and, with the chapel closing in 1967, despite Fred Barrow's best endeavours, the end of doctors' surgeries, departures of local postmen and resident priest and a gradual rise in average age through these years, we may be left with an impression of loss, decline and downward movement.

Still, Withypool maintained its tradition of providing its own entertainment with events that involved many people, generated much fun and raised money for worthwhile charities.

One excellent example is the raft race, amusingly described by Ken Almond in 1974 in its third year (3). Ken and Arthur Phillips had 10 days to design and build their boat which could float in three and a half inches of water yet be 'as unsinkable as the Titanic' – a dubious claim. Its sledge-like appearance was to allow it to be hauled swiftly over the shallow sections. With no time for sea-trials, they launched the *Pinkery Pelican* on the morning of the race and promptly capsized. After a rapid re-design they were through the central arch of the bridge and looking forward to being first to arrive at Dulverton.

However, with bruised feet, scarred shins and the bottom of the boat and ambitions severely dented they had only just made Tarr Steps by the time the winners had reached the end. 'A sympathetic marshal, who was required for duty downstream, tactfully suggested that our withdrawal would be appreciated. We didn't resist.' In fact, the course was later shortened to Tarr Steps, as most agreed it probably was a little too far . . .

The Withypool raft race achieved a degree of national fame, crowned by an appearance on the *Tony Blackburn Show*.

Mr and Mrs Pendry, the well-esteemed landlords of the Royal Oak, where several other strange projects were dreamed up, were responsible for many community fund-raising events, including this one. The home-made 'boats' were crewed by three, each being sponsored, with a prize for the boat attracting the most money and, of course, a cup for the winner. Much money was raised for various charities, including Guide Dogs, along with several departments at Musgrove Park Hospital.

Another equally eccentric charitable event was the pram race from Hawkridge to Withypool. Competitors were allowed to tip out their overgrown babies for certain stretches of steep hill, but rules were strictly enforced and the race seems to have represented a formidable challenge.

But villages as living organisms will always – indeed, must – change. And with change comes development and new growth, which we shall follow.

References

1   L Meynell, *Exmoor*, Robert Hale, 1953
2   H Eardley-Wilmot, *Withypool in the 1952 Flood*, Exmoor Review, 1981, Vol. 22, pp. 67-70
3   Ken Almond, *The Rise and Fall of the Pinkery Pelican*, Exmoor Review, 1974, Vol. 15, p. 20

Chapter 11

Natural Withypool

WITHYPOOL COMMON

Most of Withypool is moorland, an area which represents one of the few remaining true commons of Exmoor (1). Comprising 1,866 acres and rising from 850ft to 1,398ft above sea level to face generally east and north, it forms the great western rim of the parish.

Withypool Common falls into three physical regions. Bradymoor extends to about 450 acres, sloping down to the river which separates it from Brightworthy Barrows, which in turn comprises some 865 acres and is a gently sloping dome falling away to the south east into Knighton Combe. Withypool Hill, about 550 acres, lies to the east. For the most part the common's perimeter is bounded by typical Exmoor beech-topped banks.

This moorland surrounding Withypool – with its ancient history, valued hunting rights, pastoral opportunities, natural resources, isolated location and more recently its cherished landscape has – as we have shown – always been crucially important to the story of the village.

'The wide, wild open moor provided summer grazing for sheep and cattle, all-the-year-round grazing for the hardy pony stock, peat for fuel, rushes for thatching, and fern for bedding. It was the great reserve which gave much and cost nothing' (2).

And so it may be helpful at this point in our journey to raise our eyes to this 'great sweep of heather, fern and golden moor-grass' (1), to look for a moment at its history, which is both separate from, yet integral to, that of the village.

Over the centuries, many of the traditional manorial formalities, described in previous chapters, began to fall by the wayside. The owner of Withypool Common was the lord of the manor, who presided nominally over the manor court where the affairs of the common and other parish matters were regulated, as we have heard.

With the decline of the feudal system, manorial courts began to disappear, parish government passing into the keeping of the parish vestry. Custom, however, kept the relics of feudalism alive here and there, and at Withypool it devolved upon the maintenance of the common.

Across to Withypool. Photograph by Jo Minoprio.

At the end of the 18th century the lordship of the manor was shared between John Hill of Newland, who owned Higher Landacre, and Stephen Crocker of Lower Landacre. In 1843 J T B Notley purchased it as a whole, and since then the ownership of Lanacre has generally been combined with the lordship of the manor.

The court continued to meet until 1921, but the Law of Property Act 1922 put an end to copyhold. Difficult times followed: although inclosure was prevented by the 1925 Act, proper management of the common was inhibited. Motor traffic became a problem, gates were damaged and decayed and with the ravages of the war no less than 'complete disintegration' seemed possible (3).

Once again it was the users and landowners who were responsible for saving the moor. Historically, as we have heard, the commoners' rights and duties had been integral to the preservation of the landscape. Fortunately, they maintained their association. In the 19th century a large group of Withypool farmers (many a familiar name is to be seen), virtually synonymous with the old free suitors, made up the Withypool District Association.

But in the early years of the 20th century the challenge of ensuring sustainable use of the moor became more acute and in 1949 a new group, the Withypool Commoners' Association, was formed, creating a modern version of the old court and once again taking on the responsibility of protecting the living landscape through careful agricultural practice.

The iconic feature of the moor around Withypool is of course heather, but – as with other key flora and fauna characteristics – careful management underlies its survival. In those moorland areas that have been cultivated or heavily stocked, or not properly swaled, heather disappears in favour of the competing species of grasses, bracken, gorse or sedges (4).

Perhaps this helps to explain the waxing and waning of Calluna over the centuries, with heavier grazing responsible for the invasion of grasses in the forest area and the

Granfer Reed and Uncle Harry cutting turf above Knighton.
Millie Edwards Collection.

survival of the original heather on Withypool Common. With 40,000 sheep summer-pastured in the forest in 1592 (possibly even more in the 14th century) there would have been two sheep per acre – enough to destroy the cover of heather.

So we need to recall the debt we owe to the owners and users of the common, without whose diligent and disciplined approach to stocking arrangements and moorland management there would be no late summer purple on the hill to enjoy.

The importance of grazing the common has recently become recognised through substantial grants from Natural England which support graziers proportionate to their registered holdings, with a contribution to keep the heather, bracken and gorse in good order. According to Natural England, the common is one of 13 which Brussels considers top priority for support.

At the time of writing there is an effective working tripartite agreement between the lord of the manor as the landowner, the Withypool Commoners' Association – initially represented by chairman Ted Wakeham, who was succeeded by Robin Milton – and Natural England. The agreement covers, among other matters, the stocking numbers available for grazing and the expenditure of grants to manage the habitat.

Hope Bourne claimed in 1966 (1) that common rights were still held by all the farms of the parish; of these, the grazing rights continued to be valued, but others had naturally and properly lapsed. One of these was peat cutting, the last farm where it took place being Knighton.

Peat, cut up into pieces called clats, was dug on summer evenings on the hill, and the clats were set on their ends to dry, then carted down to the farm where they were built into ricks, aptly named 'Turf Barrows'. The best turf, 'Pit Turf' was the most dense and black; 'Spine Turf' from nearer the surface was lighter.

THE RIVER BARLE

Moorland may be seen as the natural surround of the village, but its spine – the thread running right through the middle – is the river. The essential role of the river in the development – and indeed the very reason for – the village has been considered. But its health and even its survival, like that of the moor, cannot be taken for granted.

As the centuries have rolled past, that which was once assumed and taken for granted becomes less certain. Moorland can be and has been damaged, resulting in loss; the natural bounties of the river can be and have been seriously depleted. Protection is now required for each.

Some 80 per cent of the salmon that spawn in the Exe, whose major tributary is the Barle, come up this river to spawn. It only takes one dog, happily splashing around, to pick up a stone in a spawning area for tens of thousands of eggs to be lost. And if changing weather patterns continue to lower water levels, the arrival of spawning salmon can be delayed, thus exacerbating shortages of eggs.

Finding the right balance between conflicting interests and activities poses an increasing challenge not just for Withypool, but for Exmoor more generally. While there is no easy answer, if a feeling of local pride can be translated into one of communal responsibility, and if a shared awareness of the fragility of these natural features can be turned into respect, then active and appropriate protection will result.

THE EXMOOR PONY

Coming across the moor to reach Withypool, the visitor will expect to see Exmoor ponies, the living icons of Exmoor. Arguments continue over whether the Exmoor Pony we recognise today has lived and thrived here since time immemorial as an ancient forest herd, or whether the distinctive Exmoor appeared later.

In any event, these ponies have been an essential part of the landscape for a very long time – whether running free, rounded up or used as a valued working animal, be it for transport, shepherding or hunting. This situation persisted until the end of the 18th century; Billingsley stating in 1798 that they had never left the moor.

As already noted, the free suitors had the right of common pasturage over Exmoor Forest for horses, which were called at various times 'Exmoor Horses', 'Horse Beasts' or 'Widge Beasts' (but never 'ponies'). The allowance was five 'beasts', those under one year old not being counted. With 37 suitors from Withypool, that meant 185 animals or, with all 52, there could have been 260 before the inclosures were made.

MacDermot gives us a picture of the horse population on Exmoor in 1777 (5). There were 164 'horses' and 165 mares when 36 'Naggs' were sold for £80. Interestingly, a description of their colours suggests that there was not

Exmoor ponies on Withypool Common. Photograph by Victoria Thomas.

the uniformity we might expect: of 81 ponies sold in three years, 33 were black, 19 grey, 17 bay, nine dun, two chasnut (sic) and one piebald.

But in 1815 they were driven off the moor. Fortunately, Thomas Acland, the last warden, took 400 to Old Ashway from where they went to Winsford Hill as the Acland (Anchor) herd. The remainder were sold to various buyers, including Mr Milton, who brought his to Withypool Hill.

Dent describes two recognisable types corresponding to these ponies (6), suggesting that the Withypool type is on the whole taller, darker, with a straight facial profile; the Acland smaller, a bright russet-brown with an s-shaped curve of face.

Among the many challenges the breed has faced over the years are John Knight's attempts to 'improve' the Exmoor with an 'Arab' (in fact a Dongola Barb), the threat posed by attempts to develop the optimal animal for pit work and their catastrophic depletion during the second world war. There are currently more than 20 herds of Exmoor Pony on the moor. Many of these are quite small, such as at Knighton, and a substantial and important proportion is centred upon Withypool.

Despite their longstanding presence, these residents of Withypool have – like their human counterparts – been through difficult times and have indeed been endangered. There has always been the problem of interbreeding, with the risk that those crucial iconic characteristics become diluted. Their superb adaptation to the moorland environment – including colouring, coat structure and conformation, along with the hidden adaptations such as the digestive capabilities (7) – can all be jeopardised.

The founding of the Exmoor Pony Society in 1921 represented one of many commendable attempts to regularise and control the identity of the breed, which continues to the present day (8).

The Exmoor Pony is then an essential part of the Withypool story in a great variety of ways, through its historical role on the moor, through its living presence in maintaining the landscape and through its vital contribution to man's use of the moor – not to mention the expectation of Exmoor's visitors. It is indeed a complex relationship that man and Exmoor Pony have enjoyed; hardly one, as Dent said, of master and servant, unless one recognises that these roles can become confused.

It would be agreeable to spend more time with the Exmoor Pony, but we must return to man – master and servant – and his village in the moor called Withypool.

References

1. Hope Bourne, *A Village of the Moor*, Exmoor Review, 1966, No. 7, p. 47
2. Hope Bourne, *Two Exmoor Farms*, Exmoor Review, 1967, Vol. 8, p. 77
3. Victor Bonham Carter, *Withypool Common A Study in Depth*, Exmoor Review, 1968, No. 9, p. 50
4. Geoffrey Sinclair, *The Vegetation of Exmoor*, Microstudy B1, Exmoor Press, 1970, p. 28
5. E T MacDermot, *The History of Exmoor*, The Wessex Press, 1911, p. 405
6. Anthony Dent, *The Pure Bred Exmoor Pony*, Microstudy A2, The Exmoor Press, 1970
7. Sue Baker, *The Survival of the Exmoor Pony*, Exmoor Review, Vol. 31, 1990, p. 67
8. Peter Green, *The Security of the Free-living Exmoor Pony*, Exmoor Review, 2015, Vol. 56, p. 94

Chapter 12

Around the Village

This story up to has now been broadly chronological, as stories often are. But as well as being about 'what happened next', stories – and indeed history itself – can be a patchwork of bits and pieces. Snippets of information, gossip, anecdotes, jokes, even exaggerated descriptions which one suspects might not be completely true – can jump out, appear or emerge, perhaps haphazardly, in relation to where you go, what you see and hear, who you meet, and what you were reminded of . . . Much of this may be not chronological at all – and possibly not even logical.

So our story of a village needs to be rounded off with – as this is at the heart of Exmoor – our own perambulation: a wandering around the place, with open eyes and ears, ready to pick up some of those fragments, which together can fill out, validate and help to complete the story.

There is not enough time for us to call in everywhere, nor can we include everything, for that would make this story of the village far too unbalanced.

We have already visited many of the places and heard something of what they have to say. But we can put aside the old papers, books and maps and set off to visit some of the places that make up Withypool and listen to what we might be told.

THE CHURCH

Although this compact building could never be said to dominate the village, its central site, raised position and striking straight pathway leading the eye upwards to its longstanding presence, all contribute to the impression that this is the most important structure.

We can see how masonry from medieval times contributes to the fabric, but cannot be sure how much of that might have been Norman, either in its original position or as recycled material. It is suggested that it is mainly 14th century (the three pointed arches of the aisle) and 15th century (the windows).

Here is a church characterised by functional

simplicity – as Hope Bourne noted, there are no shows of affluence, boasts of rich people, effigies of knights, tattered flags or war memorials. This modest moorland parish possessed no great agricultural or industrial wealth, no rich aristocrats to commemorate themselves and their families nor any prosperous merchants to leave their mark. A church reflects its congregation, so this is no more – and no less – than a simple Exmoor church, the offering of a community of hill farmers and local landowners.

Over the years work continued on both extension as well as repairs, with the original embattled and turreted tower rebuilt in 1688. A contract for extensive restoration was drawn up between 1882 and 1884, and the work eventually took place in 1887 at the cost of £150. A third of this was met by Giles Yarde and the remainder by the parishioners. The old furnishings were cleared out then, and the pulpit made by the village carpenter.

The church, then, like so much of the village, appears at first sight to be old, settled and unaltered but has in fact been much altered over the centuries, particularly latterly. Often that which seems – and in a way truly is – ancient, has been the subject of recent, not readily noticed, change. The church tower is a striking example. The photograph of Withypool which appears in Chapter 9, was taken at the turn of the 20th century and shows the church as it was then – without a tower.

The tower, which had been partly taken down, had to wait until 1902 to be re-built and even then shortage of funds was said to be responsible for the present squat structure. These works took place in 1903, costing £200. *Kelly's Directory* of 1910 states that previously there was only one bell, but five bells were then hung. However, while there is no doubt that three are modern, the third and the fifth date from 1793 and the fourth, by Thos Pennington of Exeter, from 1624. Collinson in 1791 states that there were four bells. There are now six bells which are rung regularly.

The ringing of Withypool's bells have had far reaching and indeed unexpected effects – they were held to be responsible for the departure of the king of the pixies and his family from Knighton, as we have heard (1).

A handwritten note dated April 11 1949 from the Rev Michael Etherington records that 'a cross cut deep in the stone of a tower buttress marks a spot touched by a bishop with consecration oil perhaps 700 years ago.' There is no reason to disbelieve this statement, but no confirmation has been found in any other source.

Perhaps it corresponds to the time when in 1380 the Rev Sir Richard Cadecote of 'the chapel of Wydepole' exchanged benefices with the Rev Sir Walter de Trenvelent, rector of Hawkridge, the former being installed at Hawkridge by the bishop of Exeter in the person of Sir Thomas Avenet, chaplain, under a commission from the bishop of Bath and Wells. This slightly complicated story suggests that this occasion represented an upgrading not only of Cadecote personally, but of the church of Withypool to full status, from a chapel of ease.

But over the years, the relative status of the two churches swung to and fro, for Collinson in 1792 (2) describes our church as a chapel to Hawkridge. *Kelly's Directory* from the 1860s confirms that the living was a chapelry annexed to the rectory of Hawkridge, when the Rev Joseph Jekyll MA was the incumbent.

And now they quietly co-exist, each serving its own community as part of the benefice of Exmoor, unworried by what are now happily irrelevant issues of seniority.

Inside the church on the west wall, there is a stone slab difficult to decipher from floor level, but containing words such as 'extraordinary virtue, chaste, just, prudent . . .'

'It makes you wonder where all the bad 'uns are buried', an old verger was said to declare (3).

This little story reminds us that here is a community which does not always take itself too seriously, not least when dealing with what may be considered as serious matters.

Contrary to the familiar story of a sense of loss from the amalgamation of individual parish churches into groups with a shared vicar or rector, the church in Withypool has not just retained but clearly developed its own vigour and sense of growth. There is a new noticeboard at the gate displaying up-to-date information, the churchyard is well kept, and the interior of the church clean and tidy, welcoming and decorated with fresh, particularly well-arranged flowers.

Despite sharing the rector with seven other parishes, Withypool has regular weekly services. The visitors' book, with its surprising spread of addresses from far and wide, is full of warm responses to the serenity and sanctity of the place, further witness to the life embedded in this ancient building. Interestingly, many of the people are returning to the place where their ancestors lived.

David Weir, the rector, recently wrote 'We are fortunate to live among neighbours who value community life and look out for each other and I am very grateful to live in a place where the church is rooted in that life.'

For a long time that tradition has maintained the building physically, as well as spiritually. The east window, given by their daughters Mary and Sarah, commemorates Nicholas Milton and his wife Elizabeth, who lived through most of the 19th century. Mary herself is remembered in the south window, and the organ was given by Robert Williams of Lower Blacklands. Mrs Ruby Reed, one of the last school mistresses, left a handsome legacy which transformed the finances of the church.

No doubt a great deal of the restorations, repairs and renewals to the church down the centuries were similarly paid for by local families, among whom were perhaps some of those same names. But most of those benefactors remain anonymous, their support and offerings embedded in the very fabric of the church.

A recent impressive example of this was the re-hanging of the bells in 1994, when a substantial amount of money was raised by many locals and visitors under the successful leadership of Rodney Martin. The Banks family generously allowed their tea rooms to be used for the benefit of the church that summer, when a small team sold teas and asked for donations to raise funds. In order to attract attention, a model of the church, assembled from old wedding invitations, was displayed opposite the tea rooms. Ex-evacuees, including Terence Hannan, joined enthusiastically in the fund-raising.

The church room was built in 1934 on the site of two cottages which were the former parish poor houses, built in 1855. Set in its pretty garden at the base of the churchyard, it was recently restored with the help of a legacy from Claire Norton's sister. The Norton family had originally planted the garden in Claire's memory, commemorated by a modest plaque. Claire was tragically killed in a road traffic accident in 1948 on her way to the Grand National. Her mother planted azaleas, rhododendrons and heathers which flourish today, complete with lovely mosses fluttering from the shrubs, attesting to the purity of the air.

Perhaps human love can imbue a place, for many have noticed that there is something special, even sacred, about this secluded spot in the heart of the village.

THE ROYAL OAK

The original pub was at Oak Cottage, set behind the present building, with its stables. The site of the existing inn used to be a triangle of grass, complete with a large oak tree, and parts of this building are at least 300 years old.

Withypool had other pubs – manorial court records at the beginning of the 19th century refer to meetings at an inn called the Hare and Hounds, and there was also the Cork and Bottle, which fell into ruins and is now only just discernible. In addition, the tithe award refers to the New Inn, occupied by Walter Tidboald, on a site adjacent to the shop.

As for the Royal Oak, its name suggests an origin from the 17th century, commemorating the future King Charles's flight, but perhaps the name was developed later in association with the particular oak which grew on the site.

What is certain is that this pub carries a rich history. Among its famous visitors, as we have already heard, were the author of Lorna Doone, the president of the Royal Academy and the supreme allied commander in the second world war, future president of the United States.

Over the years the pub has continued to change and develop.

There was a wooden balcony, useful for watching what was happening (who was doing what and with whom), mounting steps and an open yard to sit and drink in the open air, slightly reminiscent of today's external smoking areas. Everyone was welcome and many a community event was born here over a glass or two, including the infamous raft race and the pram race, especially when the Pendrys were the landlords. At that time it was a well-known fishing inn and Mrs Pendry was famed for her fine dinners, when she might roast pheasants and several of the well-to-do people would come and dine.

Jake Blackmore, barman at the Royal Oak. Photograph by Chris Chapman.

The Royal Oak in Maxwell Knight's time.
Rita Westcott Collection.

Jake Blackmore, in his 37th year as barman, having come for just a few months from Dulverton 'after London took over', and who may yet move further west perhaps to Brendon if the invasion persists, has many a story to tell of the pub's lurid history.

One such is that of an earlier notorious owner, a certain Maxwell Knight who when he died in 1968 was well known as a broadcaster and naturalist.

'Few were aware that this avuncular man with a brilliant rapport with animals had been one of the most important and mysterious figures in M.I.5. He was a spy-master – and Ian Fleming's model for 'M', James Bond's shadowy boss.

'In the 1930s he gathered round him an elite group of young case-officers in Department B5(b) – M.I.5.'s most secret outpost. Known as Knight's Black Agents, these men and women made a crucial contribution to Britain's readiness for the Second World War. Knight's responsibility was counter-subversion. He planted agents in the Communist Party of Great Britain, the British Union of Fascists and other pre-war extremist groups. He exposed the Communist-inspired Woolwich Arsenal Spy Ring in 1938, interned Oswald Mosely, the British Fascist leader in 1940 and in the same year uncovered a Nazi plot to prevent America's entry into the war.

'In 1927, two years after he first joined M.I.5., Maxwell and his wife, Gwladys bought the Royal Oak Inn, which they owned and ran until 1935, when Gwladys committed suicide' (4)

This awful event is itself as shrouded in mystery, as is Maxwell's own story.

Maxwell Knight, Ian Fleming's model for 'M', James Bond's shadowy boss.

The original caption to this photograph of Maxwell Knight states that he was characteristically wearing a uniform to which he was not entitled and suggests that he was a man of subterfuge, if not worse. What sort of marriage he and Gwladys enjoyed, and what secrets his wife was privy to, are among the many questions one would be interested in hearing answered.

But the fact remains that in bedroom number six she hanged herself, and – Jake insists – she haunts the place to this day. Floorboards creak as she walks, people have seen this white robed woman and a casette player has turned itself on and played music.

Down the centuries, ghosts or not, the pub has represented a centre of the village for all sorts of villagers, and been the scene of much jollity and many a wager. One such is related by Fred Milton, of his grandfather John Milton, who was a sturdily built man, exceptionally strong, and would make light of lifting heavy weights.

'One evening, when half a dozen young men were standing about on the north side of the Royal Oak in Withypool, the question arose as to whether anyone could lift the anvil (which weighed 3 cwt.) . . . One shilling was wagered . . . Well, some could lift the nose-part, others couldn't move it at all. My grandfather said: 'Give me that shilling, I'll carry the thing down and place it on the wall of Mill Bridge' – a distance of about 100 yards. To the amazement of all, he did so' (5).

THE MILL

The mill is only a short walk from the inn, as we have heard – even carrying an anvil – and was worked in conjunction with a bakery by the miller, followed by his widow until 1920. It took its water from Pennycombe Water, an easier way to pronounce Penticombe. Thought to be a much earlier name, Penticombe is a fair description of its pent-up course as it runs down to join the Barle through a deep narrow valley, passing through the old lime quarries at Newland and Chibbet Ford with its ancient stone footbridge.

Down by the Pennycombe lived the colourful character Eric Hawkins, who looked after Miss Pigott's horses, stabled at Three Weirs and Kings. His daughter Sammy Hawkins, a fearless horsewoman on the hunting field on her young bay, married an equally colourful character Len Morse, who was highly respected as kennel huntsman.

Having learnt his trade at the Beaufort, Morse worked for Miss Thorneycroft at Westerclose, and sometime at Uppington. One of his many skills was the ability to mend saddlery overnight. Sammy and Len's care of their hounds was legendary. Sammy returned to the village in the 1980s to live with her sister Sue Tarr at Barle Cottage; both sisters were tough countrywomen who worked hard to the last.

THE BRIDGE

With its six round arches Hope Bourne considered the bridge to be Withypool's best feature – the largest of the Exmoor bridges, she declared.

This lovely spot attracts people today, as it will always have done, to watch swallows and martins swoop, enjoy the quiet passage of waters, and the flow of time itself. If it's warm or sunny, children will be playing – walking awkwardly over the stones with the river washing round their legs, splashing, and fishing – as many a generation have before them. And their watching families, perhaps including several generations, will be resting on the green slopes . . .

The existing bridge dates from 1865, when the vestry meeting requested the Dulverton highway board to obtain a plan and estimate. Robert Adams's tender of £214 for a bridge of five spans was accepted, but there were problems, and after a year Adams was replaced by John Buslin and William Browne who set about building it in stone rather than brick, with an extra span.

However, in 1866 they were warned that if the quality of stone was not improved then they would have to take it all down and start again. 'The completed bridge with its six semi-elliptical arches remains as a monument to the vigilant members of the Highway Board' (6).

There used to be an older bridge about 100yds upstream, a four arched narrow bridge, whose site was marked by a group of black poplars. Eardley-Wilmot remarked in 1981 that this clump was spoilt later when the river was widened for safety. That may be when the remnant of an old narrow bridgehead on the opposite bank was removed. A large foundation stone can still be seen to this day.

Ducks and Drakes by Luke Martineau.

The river's course has been altered in other places. After the 1952 floods, its channel was diverted to the Kings side near Three Weirs to help prevent further flooding. Before that, Geoffrey Scoins noted as he walked to and from Dulverton to work, a myriad of rivulets and islands, which is now quite changed.

The islands may have gone, but Geoffrey and Miss Sheila Pigott were able to identify the 'island' where Michael Pigott asked for his ashes to be scattered in the 1980s.

THE SCHOOL

The parish school, with its grounds of four perches, was included in the tithe award of 1839. There was a school at Broadmead where the fee was 2d a week but on January 29 1874 the vestry meeting unanimously resolved to build a new schoolroom, setting up a committee of nine to do it. The site of the pound was considered, but it was built 'on Gibbs' using a rate of 1 shilling in the pound from landowners, later increased to 2 shillings 'to defray the cost of building.'

The 11 year-old Mary Huxtable (Fred Milton's mother) and her sister Lydia were among the first to register for the new school.

Children had to walk each day to school – for example, Bob Williams, born in 1910, from Brightworthy. The walk from Higher Blackland was not as far as it was from many other farms, but even that was at least two miles, often through muddy lanes.

Gordon Williams, born in 1923, describes what he wore – hobnail boots, short trousers and perhaps a long cloth coat, with a pair of lighter shoes which he changed into for school. There were times when he played truant, but it was better to ask if he could go home at dinnertime to help do something on the farm, which was an excuse to go rabbiting. (This could be quite a lucrative exercise, as we will learn from the auction of harvest produce presently.)

The bigger boys were responsible for keeping the fires made up in the winter. Gordon Williams remembered toasting his dry bread and cheese on the round old stove. If your family lived nearby, you could find some dinner there, as did Nettie Reed who would hop over the wall into her grandmother's at Way House – though unfortunately it was always mashed potato.

School treats included Christmas parties, usually

Withypool school photograph (circa 1931)

Standing, from left to right: Mrs Etherington, Fred Clatworthy (spectacles), John Williams, Gordon Williams (spectacles), Donald Hooper, Clifford Hooper, Sylvester Williams, Jack Bushen (at the back), Gordon Bushen (yawning!), Bertha Clatworthy, Dolly Brayley, Nellie Milton, Daisy Burnell, Mary Land and Pat Williams (teachers). Sitting or kneeling at the front: Miss Mary Etherington (holding a dog), Dennis Hawkins, Pat? (a gypsy), Mary Clatworthy, Joan Scoins (holding a cup), Geoff Scoins (hiding!), George Burnell, Pete Scoins (wearing a tie), Dorothy Scoins, Mabel Burnell, Mrs Reed (teacher) and Vera Lock at the Rectory, when children received a very welcome present like a game of snakes and ladders, a pop-gun or a toy trumpet. Sports days were enjoyed, as were picnic trips such as the memorable trip to Cow Castle, when they paddled in the river and later tucked into a cream tea at Picked Stones. Such journeys were by horse and cart, which were often decorated with wild flowers and foliage. And there were school plays, nativity plays and even outings to Weston-Super-Mare and Paignton by bus. One day a week the over-12s were taken to Dulverton, where there was cricket and other games for the boys, and sewing and cookery for the girls.

But numbers dwindled at the school, even though children from Hawkridge and beyond attended. At the time of Capt Gibbs's survey of 1963 there were two classes with one resident teacher and one extra from Wheddon Cross, with only nine of the 29 children from Withypool. There was a certain rivalry, with locals – 'Exmoor Ponies' – calling these incomers 'Dulverton Donkeys'. At the end, in 1970, when Mrs Richards from Porlock was the last teacher, there were only 12 children, with just one – Keith Zeitzen – living in Withypool.

Withypool school photograph taken in the late 1960s, showing some of the last pupils as the school was closed in the early 1970s. From left to right are: (back row) Caroline Mordant; Alison Thorne; Monica Severn; Peter Westcott; Jill Scoins; Richard Lock; Valerie Hurd; Sheila Thorne; Raymond Hayes; (front row) Kenneth Sinkins; Susie Scoins; Martin Thomas; Graham Sinkins; Vicky Hayes; Julian Westcott; Anne Mordant; Martyn Lock; Dawn Hayes; Diane Moyse.

THE CHAPEL

'A new Wesleyan Chapel was opened at Withypool on land given by Mr. John Hill' declared the *West Somerset Free Press* on June 17 1882. 'The scheme owed much to the work of the Rev H W Haine of the Dunster circuit. The chapel, built by Mr. Steer of Winsford, cost £300 and would seat 200.'

The older chapel was referred to in the tithe awards, whose trustees included William Dascombe, Thomas Joyce, John Burnet, William Stoate, John Tidboald and William Thorne.

The new chapel has now been converted into a residence, despite the efforts of the entrepreneurial Fred Barrow in the 1960s to keep it open. His uncle Tom, who farmed at Uppington, had been head of the chapel but with his departure and declining support it had to close in 1967.

The 1881–2 chapel was of the very best village construction, with ogee mouldings over the door and windows, Allen claims (7). 'Just within the narrow vestibule a flight of steps led up to a small gallery with four rows of seats set on a sloping floor. There was the usual central preaching platform facing a narrow aisle with seven short benches on each side.'

Methodism has a long history in Withypool, dating back to 1809 when meetings were held at Joan Kenyon's house Hillway. John Hill from Newland led the building of the first chapel three years later. Used as a carpenter's shop after the construction of the new chapel, that building has since been demolished.

'Now it is all gone, and 150 years of Methodist effort in this moorland village has come to an end' wrote Allen sadly in 1974 (7).

THE SHOP AND POST OFFICE

As with many small villages, once upon a time there were several shops. One such was the shop in the front room at Fairview, but it was Fred Barrow's that managed to survive and succeed. Taking over from his aunt Miss Blackmore, he ran it and was sub-postmaster for more than 20 years through the middle of the 20th century. After him came Mr and Mrs Jennings, Mr and Mrs Banks, and now Tony and Anita Howard.

As the picture of Withypool post office and general store suggests, Fred Barrow's shop with its pumps was a centre of village life. Here he can be seen in one of those 1960 wintry snows, with friends, neighbours, relatives

Withypool post office and general store in the time of Fred Barrow.
Maureen Batstone Collection.

William Blackmore, mounted postman. It is claimed that Withypool was the last place to maintain a postal round on horseback.
Barbara Adams Collection.

and colleagues – there was much overlap, as we will learn. Both village postmen – Fred's uncle Frank (Blackmore) and George Burnell – are ready to set off on their rounds. In the 1960s they used motorbikes, but before that the post was delivered by a postman on foot or on horseback.

The claim is that Withypool was the last place to maintain a riding round, owing to the isolation of the hill farms and the roughness of the tracks. One definite disadvantage of this arrangement was that should George happen to meet up with the hunt, the letters had to wait until the next day.

Earlier, the post office had been at the old school house, next door to Raymond's Cottage. A later resident of Raymond's was Mary Hooper, who did her post round on foot. When the roads were icy, she wore socks over her boots to prevent skidding.

Mary achieved national status on her retirement in

Mary Hooper, postmistress of Withypool.
Barbara Adams Collection.

Fred Barrow and Tony Howard in Withypool village shop and post office in 2013.
Photograph by Chris Chapman.

1949, when it was estimated that she had walked the equivalent of some four times round the world since starting in 1916. The regular postman had been called up, so she stood in on a temporary basis, but when no-one could be found for the work, she continued with the daily 10 mile round, at £2 a week.

The tramp across fields and down muddy cart tracks took her from 8am to about midday which, being considered part-time, meant that she received no pension. Despite being a smoker, Mary had remarkable energy, as *Kelly's Directory* in 1923 records that she was also sexton. When a post inspector came to the village and informed her that she was not allowed to smoke on her round, she suggested that he do the posting while she did the smoking.

Fred rose at 5am each morning, sorted the mail which arrived at 7.10am and opened his shop at 8.30am. It closed for an hour at lunchtime, with early closing on Wednesday afternoons, which allowed for a bit of rough shooting with spaniel Toby, or perhaps some fishing – 'just with a worm'.

The shop was open six days a week but if you wanted fuel Fred, being resident, was happy to serve you at any time. A taxi service was another part of the business, picked up by Fred after uncle John from Waterhouse, the previous provider, bought Higher Blackland. 'Uncle Tom's brother Cecil was farming Lower Blackland then' Fred added – yet another demonstration of what a tightly knit community Withypool was.

As well as being a post office – as the sign declares – the shop not only sold food, groceries and all sorts of household goods, but a wide range of hardware, from nails upwards. Fred was assisted by a full-time employee, Geoff Scoins's daughter Jill, who was then paid £3 a week – if Fred's memory served him right. Jill works in the shop to this day. Bread and meat came from Balsom's of Dulverton, some from Porlock and the hardware from T H Moor of South Molton. Coal deliveries from Goodlands were for the most part direct to houses, although Fred said he'd always be happy to sell it. With his strict Methodist background, however, alcohol was not sold. There was of course the well-supported pub just down the road.

He installed the first petrol pump outside the shop but then went on to build the filling station on the other side of the road. Fred Radley, of local builders Radley and Chanters, was the stonemason whose excellent work, which Fred praised, may be admired today. This enterprise had to await the arrival of mains electricity, the original pump being hand cranked. With the new pumps in place, the first was turned into serving Diesoline, as the photo shows. Fred said he always enjoyed the petrol side.

One of the shop's regular customers was Hope Bourne, who would walk the three or so cross-country miles from

Hope Bourne enjoying a cup of tea outside Withypool tea room.
Photograph by Tony Howard.

Ferny Ball just outside the parish every Friday to collect her post, send her letters, and pick up the few essentials she needed, which might include matches, a loaf, and perhaps her special treat of some chocolate.

Hope Lilian Bourne spent some 60 years of her life painting, sketching and writing about all things Exmoor, mainly centred on Withypool, her favourite place with which she will be forever associated. After several moves in her early life, she came to live in a caravan at Higher Blackland, later to rent part of Broadmead Cottage.

It was in 1970 that she finally settled to live a self-sufficient life in an old caravan at Ferny Ball in the ruins of a burnt-out farmhouse, which was to be her long-term home. She had already written and beautifully illustrated her *Little History of Exmoor*, an invaluable work upon which anyone writing a history of anywhere in Exmoor, but particularly that of Withypool, will gratefully draw.

With the passing of the years, the publication of a series of well-received books, a regular newspaper column, the making of a film in 1978 followed by another in 1997 and various consequent interviews and publicity, she achieved a fame with which she found herself not wholly comfortable.

But in Withypool this extraordinarily talented and resourceful woman, who had adopted this unusual ultra-frugal life style, was truly at home. She entered vigorously into a wide range of local and social activities, whether the hunt or visiting friends, the Exmoor Society or the flower show. Supported by many friends in the village and beyond, she found some fulfilment and contentment in her isolation, articulating in word and picture that which many of her friends (and possibly the rest of us) would like to have said or shown.

It was appropriate that, thanks to some of those friends, her latter days were spent back in the village itself, in a bungalow looking out on to the moor. She may no longer be seen buying her stamps on a Friday in the post office, but for many her vision and descriptions of Exmoor and Withypool have made such a deep impression that her presence persists.

THE TEA ROOM

Withypool tea room, recently and attractively refurbished, draws all sorts of people from far and wide. Cyclists and walkers, old and young, the vigorous and the more sedate – all may find refreshment. There is something particularly friendly here, with strangers happily engaging in conversation, a gentle feeling of coming and going and the cleanest public conveniences you will ever find; what more could a visitor ask for?

SOME HOUSES

The village not only centres on the river, but is divided by it. On the south facing side are to be found the grander houses – 'Withypool has more than its share' said Fred Barrow. Most were built as second homes by people with family traditions of holidaying here but some, like the Etherington's Newland House, were inhabited all the year round. Others, like Westerclose and Three Weirs, have in their time rendered service as guest houses or hotels.

The newer smaller houses built up the hill on the other side were for the 'working people'. Putting pressure on the rural district council was a recurrent theme in the business of the parish council. It took a long time for Tom Barrow and fellow parish councillors to get them erected in those difficult post-war years, as recurrent reports in the Free Press confirm.

Numbers 1 to 4 Hawthorn Cottages were finally built in 1950. The village survey drawn up in 1963 by Capt Gibbs RN includes an inventory of the council houses – one pre-war house, four post-war houses and four bungalows, all south of the Barle. The rents were 12s 2d, 21s 1d and 16s 10d respectively. Mr and Mrs Scoins moved into their new bungalow after their marriage in 1954 and were thrilled to have a new house.

Somehow, despite all the differences in style, size and age of the houses and a somewhat haphazard distribution, the organic growth of the built environment, for the most part reflecting a pre-planning world, the overall impression of man-made Withypool is undeniably attractive.

'You wouldn't (I am glad to say) call Withypool "picturesque". I daresay the word "picturesque" started off its life with good intentions; but it has unquestionably degenerated at least in its connotation. Some words carry shadows. The shadow of "picturesque" is "ossification"; and the shadow of that is death . . . I am glad to think that "picturesque" is not the first word that comes to mind when thinking of Withypool. It looks something much better than that. It looks pleasantly and agreeably functional; and it was made for the most part in an age when being functional didn't necessarily imply being ugly' (3).

There are cottages on the north side and scattered throughout the village, some of which have been holiday homes for generations of the same family. One example is the Martineau family, with this pleasant description from Luke, which can speak for many others.

'I have been coming on holiday to Exmoor since I was born . . . My grandfather bought our cottage which was very basic in the early fifties - no electricity, two

up two down – because he liked hunting and fishing. Little did he suspect his great grandchildren would be splashing around in the river sixty summers later, enjoying the simple pleasures of walking on the moor, buying ice creams and nets from the village shop and trying to catch 'taddlers' (our word for minnows) all afternoon . . . the continuity of our collective memories are important . . .' (8).

Some decrepit cottages were demolished, such as Quick's Cottage, described in 1977 as situated at the top of Desmond Longe's garden. In the mid 19th century it was occupied by the family of James Quick, a blacksmith who charged 7s 6d (35p) to shoe a horse, and carried on shoeing after he went blind. Others were cleared to make a site for new building, as with The Palace – to be explained.

Many another house has its own interesting history.

According to the 1891 census, Mill Cleave Cottage, home of John Steer, a retired blacksmith (82), his wife Mary (73) and Jane Crocker (39), their daughter-in-law, had a fourth inhabitant. He was the only person in Withypool at that time to have been born in London and was described as 'Boarder'.

Bertie Thomas, then four years old, arrived in the village under a veil of secrecy. Later he was apprenticed to farmer John Williams, moving to Swansea before the first world war. The strange circumstances persist, for apparently the documents that were left for safe-keeping with 'a local vicar' disappeared, and other relevant records in a Welsh Records Office were lost in a blitz. In 1992 the *Tiverton Gazette* reported that a man claiming to be his son had laid claim to a large estate, as the illegitimate grandson of Edward VII.

Hamiltons represents another example of a cottage being demolished to make way for a bigger, better house. John Milton (son of Samuel from Waterhouse) built 'The Palace', paying £1,000 in gold sovereigns, which raises interesting questions. The date 1875 is carved in Roman numerals in stone over the porch. It has a great store of anecdotes. Not only was this where the Munnings stayed, but it was the home of Miss Shoppe, who had an Italian cook (pronounced locally with an emphasis on the 'I', as in 'eye'). It was said that there was always an enticing smell of simmering onions, which was probably in those days remarkable, if not positively exotic.

The redoubtable Miss Rathbone was a master of foxhounds (the Cottesmore), which happens to be a tradition at Hamiltons continued to this day. She served in the Women's Auxiliary Air Force (WAAF) in the second world war, was an excellent seamstress and cared for evacuees. Buying the house from the Miltons in 1970, she renamed it The Hamiltons, and contributed generously to village life.

Harvest produce auction at the Royal Oak.
From left to right are: David Hosegood; Mike Bradley; Geoffrey Scoins; the Rev John Atkin.

Miss Rathbone was famous for setting her heart on particular items when harvest produce was auctioned – so much so that locals would somewhat mischievously push the price up to absurd levels to see how far she might go. It is said that on one occasion she paid £100 for a rabbit. Perhaps this was no more than a good-humoured way to contribute to village funds.

This striking character was another who first came to Withypool as a young girl, to settle here in later life, although by then disabled after an accident.

Miss Rathbone's story reminds us that Withypool is definitely a place to which people return in later life, if not in death. For example, in 2013 Muriel Bilkey was brought back to be buried in the churchyard. She had lived at South Hill; her family the Hoopers may have left in 1941, but she returned, to be buried with her ancestors. Her family had farmed at Well, but that was another house which was destroyed by fire, and never rebuilt.

Also like many others, Miss Rathbone had been drawn to Withypool by the hunting. Her uncle owned Hill Cottage with a stable yard which Reg Stanton acquired in the 1980s. With his wife Jill he ran Hawthorne stables for hacking and livery. Miss Rathbone built the handsome brick house next door for her groom in the 1950s. The yard has now gone, with the appropriately named Harriers built in its stead.

She was a fine Bridge player, organising parties and playing to win, as she did at the flower show. She proudly claimed she was a 'jug baby' (that is, so premature that she could fit in a jug) so was fed, as was the custom then with prematurity, on brandy and milk. After a long and colourful life, she ended her days in an old people's home, happily surviving once again on brandy and milk – enjoying the joke.

Some of the houses on the north side, especially those down by the river, remained rather primitive. Bridge House for example had been condemned by the sanitary inspector from Dulverton some years before the flood, although it remained inhabited. In October 1952 the inspector wrote again to say that 'it is such a state that it cannot be allowed to be re-occupied, neither in my opinion could it be brought up to a reasonable standard of fitness.' Mrs Reed challenged his demand that it remain vacant, but he insisted that it was totally unfit to live in, issuing an order to that effect.

The state of this particular house cannot have been unique. Although the vestry meetings show that efforts had been made to bring water to the village at least from 1914, mains water had only arrived in 1930, when two standpipes brought it from a spring near Portford Bridge, thanks to the Heywood family.

There must have been a marked degree of rural poverty, which perhaps explains the not very kind comment of the father of a contemporary Withypool resident – 'You couldn't pay people to live in Withypool.'

Fred Barrow described this awareness of the contrasting social distinctions, as it was reflected in the doctors' lists – Dr Collins looking after the better off, while Dr McKinney was seen as 'the working man's doctor'. Later, in the 1980s Dr Woodman treated everyone and then, like many other branch surgeries, the surgery in the village hall ceased in the 1990s.

But it was Dr McKinney who looked after Geoffrey Nicholson, from a very prosperous family, who was suffering from serious depression and eventually killed himself in 1935. Like many others, he had come to Withypool when young and, wanting to return, decided to build his own house here in 1927.

Westerclose was said to be the one of the best-built houses in the village, the South Molton builder Sanders using stone quarried from an adjacent field. There was a staff of five and a nurse – Paddy Moynham, a delightful and cheerful Irishman – who lived in, to look after him. Poor Dr McKinney stated that having to section (enforced psychiatric hospitalisation) his friend and patient was the worst thing he had to do in his life. Paddy married after the war and settled at Oliver's Cottage (10).

THE FARMS

In 1966 Hope Bourne still felt able to state that agriculture continued to be the life of Withypool (10). Whether one would make this claim some 50 years later is open to debate. Certainly, it remains the main industry, is key to preserving the landscape, and is probably the primary employer.

However, it could be argued that the leisure industry (excuse the oxymoron) – incorporating as it does holiday visitors, second home owners and in general people enjoying the national park, not to mention the retired and those involved in supporting all the foregoing – has taken over as the main activity.

In any event, the scattered hill farms – 16 were listed by the Dulverton Rural District Council in 1961 – represent the backbone of both these activities. All are old, if not of ancient origin, with, in Hope's fine phrase, centuries of quiet history behind them, and untold years of endeavour and striving with moor and storm and sullen soil. No-one took it upon themselves to document their story. Those hard-working farmers had more pressing things to get on with, combined with a certain modesty as to the importance of the various activities involved. Who would want to know anyway?

Most of the original farms have survived – many still with land, some with a little, but maintaining their origin perhaps through horses. Others have evolved into dwellings, that is to say primarily places to live in.

And of course there were other farms, little houses and habitations now melted back into the ground from which they grew; some have left a definite mark, some a hint, and others, like their occupants, no evidence at all.

HIGHER AND LOWER BLACKLAND FARMS

These ancient farms – referred to in pleas of the forest as long ago as 1270 – have already been described (11) and have figured frequently in our history. Some of them have been shown as a classic example of a Saxon settlement, others – with their improvements – a sign of increasing prosperity, and others a centre of mining activity which, if the geography had been slightly different, might have transformed not just Withypool, but the wider area.

Gordon Williams, born in 1923 the youngest of six, tells us graphically in his 1993 memoir of *Exmoor Farming – The Way It Was* what it felt like to live at Higher Blackland with its 280 acres in the early years of the 20th century.

There was no electricity or running water indoors. An open gutter brought water from Bradymoor Bog for washing, and a pump produced drinking water unless it dried up, 'when water had to be fetched from a running spring a couple of fields away by bucket or churn.' The

Fred Blackmore loading hay at Newland.
Barbara Adams Collection.

lavatory was at the bottom of the courtyard in a little house, sensibly equipped with both a large seat and a small one, a supply of old newspaper and a running stream underneath.

Killing the pig, thatching the hayricks and sheep dipping (under the local policeman's supervision) are just a few of the regular events in the annual calendar we learn about.

When he was only 14 years old, with just a 19 year-old brother, his sisters all having left home and both parents dead, his uncle decided that the two boys did not know enough about farming to keep their farm, so it was sold and Gordon went to work on another farm.

In the time of the three Common sisters, horses were still at work in the 1950s at Lower Blackland Farm, which deeply impressed a visiting writer (3).

John Blackmore bought the 200 acre farm when the remaining sisters left after the bad winter of 1963. It was as well that he liked a challenge, for it was not in good condition; instances of the sisters' primitive way of life included widespread vermin, and dead kittens behind the hearth. He sold off some of the land and the house and built a bungalow, but he himself had to move away in 1967 when his wife died.

This story, like many others, shows how – perhaps despite settled appearances – ownership of farms and houses in Withypool has often changed, with land separated from original farms, other parcels bought and new buildings appearing.

It also reminds us that upland farming in recent times, no less than in the very earliest times, continues to be a hard and demanding occupation, calling for energy, family support and enterprise. And it shows how a spell of bad weather can tip the balance.

WEATHERSLADE

A powerful presence here is that of Fred Milton, who farmed at Weatherslade all his life, helped re-establish the common after the second world war and played a leading part in preserving and protecting the Exmoor Pony. In contrast to other farmers, he also wrote a fascinating memoir upon which I have drawn.

The buildings of Streetwall, where his great-great-great-grandfather Robert lived in the 18th century have, like others, long since disappeared. He cultivated several acres of oats and barley and an acre or so of wheat for bread. The hard work, patience and persistence required to do this with the primitive technology then available is impressive. His brother Samuel was if anything even more successful at Foxtwichen (see below).

The eldest of Samuel's 10 children was Betsy, Fred's grandmother who married her cousin John in 1860. They lived at Dadhayes, bringing up six children, the third boy being Fred's father John Milton, a sturdily built man of whose strength we learnt when we looked at the history of the Royal Oak.

Haulage with horse and cart meant journeys from Porlock Weir to Newland Lime Kilns – on a good day, twice – carrying coal and lime, which he distributed to many local farms. He delivered the stone for the new Withypool bridge being built by William Brown of Porlock from Withypool Hill, and was proud to have the honour of being the first to drive his cart over it.

From Fred comes the famous story of his grandfather's visit to London. John ordered a new suit from the local tailor Mr Tudball, who conducted his business at the Royal Oak, and new boots from Mr Quartley, who lived at Rose Cottage, down the road from the inn.

Fred walked the 10 miles to the railway to catch a train to arrive finally at his aunt Anne's in London. Settling down for the night, he blew out the gas light, not realising that the gas needed turning off. Luckily auntie smelled it and rushed in before disaster struck. The next day, walking down a quiet street, he attracted the comment from a passing cockney startled by the noise from his iron-shod boots 'My word, Mister, what a pair of boxes.'

Auntie Anne kindly took him along to a local shoe shop to buy a new pair.

Fred's father Charles came to live at Weatherslade aged 13, where he learned about horses from John Tucker. While horses remained his main work – he sold ponies at Bampton and Bridgwater, and he himself must have ridden thousands of miles – he farmed at Weatherslade, latterly with his son, Fred.

Fred tells how Charles responded to a neighbour who lived further down the hill, complaining about the water from the Miltons' fields 'Father calmly replied, "water does run downhill, Sir."'

For his part, Fred lived at Weatherslade, riding from an early age and using his pony to go to school, which was left at George Hooper's stable at the rear of the

Royal Oak. Fred remembered how during the first world war much land had to be ploughed up for extra food production, which was all done by horses, and he shepherded sheep on the moor. He also recalled that there were still wild cats which moved with a slinking gait on the far side of Room Hill in the early 20th century, which may yet be associated with those more recent stories about the Exmoor Beast.

FOXTWITCHEN

Foxtwitchen was sometimes called Leys or Leighs in the tithe award. Fred Milton's ancestor Robert had an elder brother Samuel, who farmed at Foxtwitchen and was a very successful corn grower, selling 1,000 bushels of oats at South Molton in one season, with enough kept to feed the cattle over the winter. He also grew several acres of turnips for the sheep.

Samuel was educated and used his literacy to good effect, writing letters for local people and helping set up the school. Samuel owned Broadmead House, part of Weyhouse, a cottage adjoining the churchyard, and Waterhouse where they later went to live. His wife died, but he remarried and fathered a further family of seven.

The prolific Samuel, with 17 children altogether, who later moved to farm at Waterhouse, finally dying at Long's Cottage, is a good example of Withypool life in the mid 19th century – not only with inter-marriage, but with large families (called 'long families') and, despite an apparent permanence, many moves from one farm to another.

John Bawden, son of the famous huntsman Ernest, who farmed at Foxtwichen was a keen staghunter, acting as a guide to visitors.

In 1938 Herbert Norton, a first world war veteran, and his wife Joan, attracted by the romantic sounding name, bought the farm of some 120 acres, built a new house and played a vigorous role in village life. Later, as has so often happened in Withypool, the farm and land was sold and parts were separated, although in this case the parts were subsequently reunited. The tradition of riding at Foxtwichen continues.

UPPINGTON

The 1841 census gives an idea of the number of people living in a house. The cottages may have been filled to bursting, but the bigger houses could be as full. Here at Uppington lived John Leigh with his 25 year-old wife and baby daughter, plus grandmother Leigh, as well as five labourers, an apprentice and three others. In 1891 the census showed eight inhabitants.

Like many others before and since, Miss Evelyn Bent came to Withypool to hunt. She shared Uppington with the Barrows, who worked for her. She then built Bigmoor, into which she moved. Many families stayed at Bigmoor, including the Nicholsons in 1927 while Westerclose was being built. They were able to keep an eye on the work, using binoculars.

Miss Bent provided the horse and cart for Tom Barrow to run a milk round, which must have posed problems

Riders in Withypool c1920, showing Miss Pigott second from left.
Margaret Hankey Collection

with the steep hills, not to mention the competition it would have run into with the other more established rounds, such as Vera Lock's from Fir Tree Farm. Vera's round was certainly well established as she had begun by delivering telegrams on her pony, building up the milk round later on. Her father Evan originally worked as a farrier and, being a first world war veteran, always wore putties.

Uppington was a rambling farmhouse where the main staircase was Georgian, various ladders being used elsewhere. Above the stables there was one leading to the hay loft where an old man lived, and the bathroom was in a shed. Perhaps it was little wonder that there followed a series of unsatisfactory tenants, including a psychiatrist. By the time the Bidies inherited Uppington in 1971 'it was a wreck', which took 18 months to sort out.

KINGS FARM

Kings was an old farm with extensive stabling and grazing, which the Pigotts used as a hunting box to stable most of their horses, when they owned both Kings and Three Weirs. Miss Pigott lived at Three Weirs, which her father had remodelled in the 1920s. It was always said that there were flies by the river at Kings.

Geoffrey Scoins would reminisce about the wonderful barn at Kings where village dances were held. Unfortunately it was pulled down after the war.

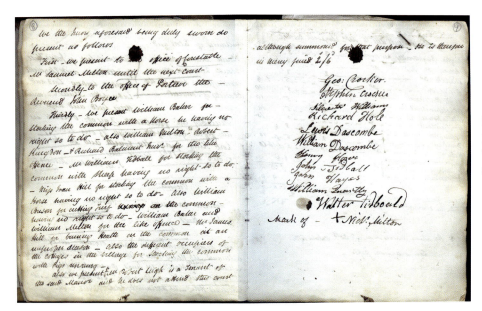

Proceedings from the court leet of Michaelmas 1827, showing Nick Milton's signature with an 'x' when his colleagues were able to write their signatures in full.

WESTWATER

Fred Clatworthy took over this family farm of some 200 acres (including moorland) in 1954. Along with sheep and cattle rearing, fields of mangolds, swedes and cabbages were grown. Happily, and unusually, this farm – which used to be in Winsford parish – remains intact and farmed by the same family to this day, and seems destined to continue with the latest generation committed to the agricultural tradition.

LANACRE

'Here the Barle runs very fair and friendly in its valley, and the moor is vast and big about you. There is a feeling of remoteness and seclusion about this valley . . . an air, too, of secrecy, as though somewhere in the folds of these hills something is hidden, some secret, some wisdom maybe, which it would be well to seek' (3).

The importance of Lanacre has already been well established throughout this story, with its early manorial status and many subsequent historical connections.

Nicholas Milton, Fred's great-great grandfather, at the age of 36 with four children, became the tenant of Lower Landacre in 1807. True to the spirit of the times, he was an energetic man, with a plan to reclaim land and bring it into good cultivation. He built many banks on Bradymoor and although the Inclosure Act of 1815 prevented him planting beech hedges, he succeeded in finishing a number of fields.

His son Nicholas, who inherited his father's love of Exmoor ponies, took over both Higher and Lower Landacre. The new owner, Mr Notley decided to repair and renew Lower Landacre at the expense of Higher, with much help from Nicholas, who was very proud when he entered 'the new house'.

Although Nicholas Milton was illiterate, he was keen that his daughters should be educated. One day he asked his eldest what she'd learnt at school. She told him that the world was round, it moved on its axis and revolved every 24 hours. 'That can't be true, because Ham Gate was over by Comers Cross when we came to live at Landacre over forty years ago, and it's still there now.'

The various lords of the manor have been noted in previous chapters, but we can now bring it up to date with Peter Hudson, lord of the manor for 35 years, farming sheep and cattle. Another master of foxhounds, he not only loved his hunting but, with his wife Jane, was a keen gardener. They both enjoyed fishing. On one famous occasion, when they were both about 80 years old, Jane caught a large salmon by herself but was unable to land it. Her husband went to help and eventually they succeeded. It was a fine catch, and a happy way to remember this couple whose family continue the tradition of lord of the manor of Lanacre.

The bridge is first mentioned in documents of 1610, and in 1621 a rate was raised for its repair, when it was known as 'Long Acre Bridge' – more meaningful than its present day name, which continues to be spelled in a wonderful variety of ways (2).

Estimates for, and accounts of, its repair between 1816 and 1819 record the need for much timber and many man and horse hours to complete the works, which included partially diverting the river. There were more repairs – in 1829, for example, £30 19s 8d was spent – with continuing care down the years since.

And rightly so. For many, this is a quintessential Exmoor spot, a scene of happy riverside days from childhood holidays, so much more than just a bridge, with its position, natural sweep and comfortable placing in the landscape. It has captured the heart and imagination of generations of visitors, figuring not only in many a family snapshot, but also in R D Blackmore's Lorna Doone when Tom Faggus escapes from justice (Chapter XLVII).

The Final Salmon: Jane and Peter Hudson at Lanacre in 2007. Photograph by Jo Minoprio.

KNIGHTON

Tucked away slightly mysteriously down its winding lane, this ancient farm is shrouded in its own curious legends, as we have heard. Before the road was constructed, it was described as a rough place, with big rocks scattered about the yard.

Another reminder of the primitive state and isolation of this farm comes from Millie Reed (now Edwards) who describes how, soon after the first world war, her grandfather decided that his wife needed to learn how to shoot to defend herself against possible marauders who then roamed the countryside. So he set up a lighted candle at one end of the long kitchen table and using a blunderbuss, taught her how to put it out. That kitchen wall would have been well peppered.

Frederick Reed himself must have been quite a man – short in build, he was considered right for mining, walking daily to work at Wheal Eliza from the age of 13 to earn 9d a week. Despite the inevitable lung troubles and a duodenal ulcer which necessitated an operation in faraway Bristol, he went on to farm at Knighton for many years, living into his eighties.

The story of his walk to Dulverton to register his new baby daughter's birth gives an idea of the measure of his doggedness. Fred had encountered the abbreviated name of Nettie when he was in Wales but the registrar refused to accept this name, insisting it be changed to Nestor or something more acceptable to the authorities. Fred stood his ground, threatening to return to Withypool without registration. He won of course and Nettie was duly registered.

When Nettie was born the nurse from the village had to hold the pony's tail to be guided through the deep snow to the farm. So cut off was Knighton that she had to stay with the Reeds for some two weeks.

However, Fred proved himself to be an entrepreneur, buying Bridge House and Cottage for £50 in 1905 and renting them out. Although renting, not owning his own farm, he improved Knighton to such an extent that by the 1920s his paying guests were to include Lord and Lady Russell of Liverpool.

Later it was this farm that was one of the first to take delivery of a tractor, his being a Fordson, registration number FYD 816.

As we have heard, for many Withypool people, residents as well as farmers, having paying guests became an increasingly important activity and source of income, as the 20th century progressed and the Reeds proved to be very popular hosts.

More latterly, it was here at Knighton on the edge of the moor that the Dulverton West would often meet. And today this is the base for the acclaimed Knightoncombe herd of Exmoor ponies (H8), originating in 1974 from two fillies and an older mare from Miss Dashwood of Clayford, under the care of the Mitchells.

NEWLAND

The importance of this farm has already been noted, with its number of attached suits – at three – being greater than any other single farm. As explained in Chapter 4, a suit was a set of commoner's privileges attached to their properties. As the centuries passed and land was bought and sold, some farms were enlarged while others disappeared completely. This led to several farms having more than one set of privileges attached to them, in direct correlation to the prosperity and economic potential of that holding.

There have been various mentions of Newland in our story down the centuries as, for example, with the 19th century John Hill who built the Methodist chapel and the 17th century John Hyll (sic), who worked for the notorious Boevey for 20 years. Hill left shortly before the dispute about the ownership of the commons, appearing as a witness for both sides, and so impressed the clerk that he was described as 'gentleman' (11). Perhaps this was as much due to his substantial estate, which included four properties in South Molton and elsewhere, as well as well-endowed Newland and other tenements locally.

The Hills (howsoever spelled) achieved remarkable continuity, holding this farm from 1657 to 1920, father succeeding son, John and James, John and James until in 1810 the second James who had no children left it to a nephew, another John. Then it passed to his sons, John and James. Nearly all of them bequeathed money to the poor of Withypool (12).

Their wills give at least two illuminating insights into social history – with the family ramifying and growing increasingly prosperous.

First, in the specific itemisation of the wills in the 18th century: 'the feather bed on which I usually lay . . . two of my best brass milk pans, one Oak Box marked with the letter E with all those things lockt up in the same', whereas later in high Victorian times there is a long list including mahogany chairs and tables, a piano and a large furnace.

Second, in the care with which the expected needs of married and unmarried daughters were carefully considered in the wills. So in the late 18th century the unmarried Joan was left the gold-laced silk gown and a full range of the best household items (the best bed, the copper boilers, the large oak table, four of the best chairs) as she was most likely to stay at home, and to live alone. Her married sisters however inherited annuities, along with various items such as 'my best laced handkerchief', 'my large silver shugar Castor' and 'my old black Quilted Coat my best Stays my red Gown and black silk Hat'.

It was (fittingly) a John Hill who finally sold Newland in 1920 to the Bawden brothers for £3,170 in 1920.

Rector Etherington built a Californian style ranch house for his American wife, complete with long stone corridors, which members of the Colvin family found 'always bitterly cold'. The Etheringtons are well known to us now, with their many contributions to village life, ranging from work with Exmoor ponies to their pastoral ministry, from amateur dramatics to social occasions. A churchwarden of that time commented that it was only with their (and the Nortons') departure that the congregation realised that funds had to be raised for the church, these two families having quietly supported the church financially for a long time.

WATERHOUSE

Barbara Adams (Blackmore) was a child here in the war when the farm had some 40 acres, where many troops were camped. She remembers how American soldiers helped themselves to the potato harvest, pushing the stalks of the plants back into the ground to pretend nothing was amiss. They also stole the dog.

Millie Edwards recalls the Royal Welsh Fusiliers as sharp shooters, picking off a lamb on one occasion. Her enraged father complained to their commander, and was properly compensated. Another time some of them stole eggs from under a sitting hen, which amused Millie, thinking how she would not have wanted to eat those particular eggs.

Early in the war, one Sunday she was standing near the church when a group of Scottish soldiers passed. The little Exmoor girl was amazed to see men, let alone fighting men, in skirts. One came over to her and said that he had a little girl just like her at home. She still wonders all these years later if he ever saw his little girl again.

BRIGHTWORTHY

John Pring was a recent chairman of the Withypool Commoners' Association and has been a much appreciated source, with Tim Davey, of valuable historical material in this project.

There are some sad episodes in the past which remind us in these relatively secure and healthy times of the hardships our ancestors had to deal with.

In 1851 three generations of the Thorne family lived here, with the Dallyns (William and Sarah and nine children) occupying it in 1879. Sadly, in 1887 four of them died from diphtheria, which caused 10 deaths in the village. It was said to have originated from the contamination of the old well in the school house. Fred Milton's aunt Elizabeth Huxtable came to Brightworthy to help, but carried the disease back to Hill Cottage (known as New Buildings) as a result of which her mother Susan aged 55, along with her two sisters, Lydia aged 16 and Thursa aged 24, all died.

Poor Fred's grandfather went to three funerals in three consecutive weeks.

In 1890 William Milton lived here with his three sons, all born at Brightworthy. Fred, the youngest, killed himself by jumping in the river; another was burnt to death in one of several dreadful Withypool fires.

HILLWAY

Another fatal fire happened here when, in the mid 1980s, early on April 5 Mrs Falcon died, her husband managing to escape by jumping from an upstairs window. The tragedy was compounded by the first fire engine becoming jammed in the narrow road, thus preventing others attending. All the contents of the house were lost, including at least one Munnings painting. Forensic experts found the damage so complete that they could not identify the seat of the fire.

The site of the old house is now a pretty garden, with the adjacent cowshed adapted into a dwelling by the Strattons. John Land, who farmed here with his wife Mary and seven children in the early 20th century, wrote a diary which represents a rich description of life in Withypool from 1913 until 1940.

We read how, after renting the farm for a few years, he bought Hillway in 1920 with a deposit of £45, having ridden to Roadwater where he had to stay the night unexpectedly with a large sum of money in his possession.

He contracted annually with the surveyor at Dulverton (not always successfully) to maintain local roads, which involved quarrying and carting the stone. With his large family and those external commitments, as well as all the challenges of hill farming, he still found time for bell ringing and regularly attended chapel. He must have been a man of great energy and resource.

When his first daughter Ann married, he noted that they were all able to attend the wedding. His second daughter Mary, who lived at Hillway until she was 32 when her father finally sold the farm, started teaching in the school at Withypool at the age of 16 and later won a scholarship to train at Taunton.

HALSGROVE

John Thorne and his wife Sarah (aged 46) with their nine children, ranging from the age of 25 to one, were tenants here at the time of the tithe award. The poor man was later killed by his bull. The 1891 census records that George Webber farmed Halsgrove, with his two daughters Bessie and Mary Ann, listed as 'scholars'.

With its well-balanced blend of pasture, arable, meadow and woodland this has always been a prosperous farm, with a greater value in the tithe award than, for example, Lower Landacre which follows it in the document.

More recently, Major Hambro moved from the splendid Coldham Hall in Suffolk to Halsgrove, showing prize-winning Herefords bred by his farm manager Leslie Rayson.

SOUTH HILL

George Hayes was born here. He later joined the Metropolitan Police and became bodyguard to Queen Victoria, saving her life during a state occasion at Windsor by grabbing the assailant's revolver. She rewarded him with a gift of £50 and a cane, which at the time Fred Milton told the story in 1977 was still in the family's possession.

Poor Mary Burgess, 'a domestic', was burned to death in her bed in a fire in 1858, along with Grace Shapland, Matthew Shapland and John Hayes (aged, respectively, 12, 22 and 63).

More happily, for many years Mr Baker had a campsite by the river which was a rural idyll for holiday makers, who returned year after year.

NEW HOUSE

This farm – its 'new' name rightly suggesting its age, dates back to 1327 when it appears in records as Niwehalle. In 1607 we find it documented as Newe House when it was glebeland belonging to Hawkridge church. The farm was still glebe in 1833 and later became a riding stable, for which it was well placed on the rim of the moor. There were even hounds here – a motley pack, which farmers would sometimes have for their own rough hunting.

BATSOM

This is another ancient farm – another of the free suitors – which has changed ownership several times in recent history. With these changes, parcels of land were sold off separately. So after some of the original 90 acres were sold to Great Bradley, there remain only about 30.

But, as has always been the case with immigration over the centuries, it is often the new arrivals, such as those who came here, who join the community with enthusiasm and commitment, ensuring continuity and infusing vigour.

WORTH FARM

This farm, straddling Winsford, Hawkridge and Withypool, owned by Squire Bellew, was in 1888 tenanted by yet another ancestor of Fred Milton, Rebecca Huxtable who married Jim Hayes. They had nine children, one of whom, Harry, carried on until 1916 when Alfie Burnell took over. Of that family of nine, two went to New Zealand.

Their brother Fred was accidentally shot in the abdomen in 1926 when, holding his gun in his lap, his sister Gladys brushed past him in the kitchen. The poor man died 'in great agony'.

John Quartley of the Hayes family was sexton.

John Quartley, sexton, in 1912. Edna Hayes Collection.

KITRIDGE

Not every farm is ancient with long past stories of struggle and, at least sometimes, sadness. When 60 acres of land high on the north-western edge of the village came up for sale in 1993, Mike and Gina Rawle applied for planning permission to build a farmhouse to go with the land. Despite opposition at higher levels, the parish council gave their support. Against the odds, the Rawles were granted permission.

It took nearly three years before their home was ready and during that time the couple and their two young children lived in a caravan on the site without electricity or running water. Gina looks back to that period of their lives with 'amazement' at how they coped. She had an office job at the time which required her to turn up for work looking reasonably smart – a tall order under the circumstances.

This story of modern times – with its demonstration of the good sense and patience of the community of Withypool (on this occasion, its parish council) in the face of superior opposition, the determination and persistence

Mike Rawle haymaking, Kitridge Farm. Photograph by Chris Chapman.

of farmers (which down the centuries, this history bears witness to) and the continuing vitality of agricultural work, essential to the life of this village, must be an appropriate one with which to end our perambulation around Withypool farms.

References

1. J B Smith, *1st Report on Dialect and Folklore*, Trans. Devon Ass. Advmt Sci., 143, p. 402
2. John Collinson, *The History and Antiquities of the County of Somerset*, 1791, reprinted 1983, Alan Sutton
3. Laurence Meynell, *Exmoor*, 1953, Robert Hale
4. Anthony Masters, *The Man Who Was M: The Life of Maxwell Knight*. Blackwell, 1984
5. F C J Milton, *The Miltons of Withypool*, Exmoor Review, 1968, Vol. 9, pp. 63-68
6. David Greenfield, *Some Exmoor Bridges*, Exmoor Review, 1987, Vol. 28, p. 30
7. N V Allen, *Churches and Chapels of Exmoor*, Microstudy F1, The Exmoor Press, 1974
8. Luke Martineau, *An Exmoor Gallery*, Exmoor Review, 2013, Vol. 54, p. 17-21
9. Bruce Heywood, *A Singular Exmoor Man*, Hector Heywood Ryelands, 2012, p. 72
10. Hope Bourne, *A Village of the Moor*, Exmoor Review, 1966, No. 7, p. 47
11. Hope Bourne, *Two Exmoor Farms*, Exmoor Review, 1967, No. 8, p. 74
12. Hazel Eardley-Wilmot, *Exmoor*, Exmoor Books, 1990

Much material on the farms has been drawn from a narration by Fred Milton at Brightworthy on September 26 1977, via John Pring and Tim Davey, which is gratefully acknowledged.

Chapter 13

Past, Present and Future – People and Place

And so we need to settle back, after our own perambulation, perhaps over a pint in the Royal Oak or a cup of tea in the tea room.

The place tells us as much about the people, as the people do about the place. We have travelled in time and space, and find ourselves affected by many responses – our own, and those of others.

The initiative of early settlers, the determination of those who established the village, the persistence of many a farmer, the courage and leadership of wives, sisters and daughters, the goodwill and contributions of later arrivers . . . kindness to visitors, patience in the face of adversity and good natured tolerance of enforced change – one is left with an awareness of all these.

So much has happened, so many lives lived, so much achieved – if nothing else, history teaches respect, if not outright admiration.

But we are now in the present.

In 1961 Capt Gibbs wrote that Withypool was a dying village.

He acknowledged that the farms and much of the farming community remained, 'but due to mechanisation, farming offers little to the village people. Therefore, as there is no other local industry, the children are drifting away from the village as they grow up.'

There were then only nine children of primary school age in a population of 179. He was concerned that there was an increasing proportion of single people in houses, and 'another possible disturbing fact is the gradual influx of well-to-do part time or weekend residents. This is regretted by such Withypool people as have discussed the matter with the writer of this Review, on the grounds that the whole balance of the community is being disturbed.'

Capt Gibbs calculated that about half the village was in employment, with about 16 per cent retired. Some 30 years later, Tim Davey reckoned that only just over a third were economically active, with the retired comprising some 40 per cent.

A more recent assessment would probably show an extension of these developments.

In a way, these trends give hope for the immediate future. In today's more comfortable and well-endowed society with a greater proportion of retired people, there is less need for providing work prospects. Young people may well move to where their work is, but experience shows that many return, and recent history as described here also shows that older people returning to the village bring commitment, enthusiasm and, yes, new life.

One answer for him was the development of small rural industries. Interestingly, there are some noteworthy developments.

Even though usually hidden from general view, there

Withypool village from the common. Photograph by Chris Chapman.

are many very productive gardens, and all sorts of creative activity goes on. The visitor would appreciate that farming and its multiple associated occupations and crafts remain the mainstay of the economy, but might be surprised to learn about some of the other productive activities that take place in Withypool, even if they knew that there were once mines here.

In an attractive, traditional-looking agricultural building at the bottom of the village a highly skilled ex-aero craftsman engineers precise components for a huge range of purposes, ranging from bed knobs for a Russian oligarch's multi-million pound yacht to key parts of the wonderful Winston Churchill memorial gates in the crypt of St Paul's Cathedral. Examples of Michael Witney's work are to be found from Bampton to New York. Despite replaced joints and ongoing arthritis, like many an old country craftsman before him, he continues to work because he loves it.

A more traditional craft is practised at Batsom farm where Sue Wakeham produces charcoal, attractively packaged and for sale appropriately at the village shop.

Charcoal burning was one of the important activities here and elsewhere for many centuries, with areas of woodlands specifically set up for it. In fact, the maintenance of woodland to make charcoal on a continuing basis underpinned the appearance of the landscape.

At Batsom, through research, observation, instruction and practice Sue has worked out the principles involved, and understandably takes great pleasure in coppicing, gathering, firing her kiln and producing this ancient but still very useful high quality fuel source, with impressive green credentials. And she has learnt much about the nature, history and structure of the local woods. At present, this activity is probably not economical, but the prospect of combining a group of producers into a cooperative might well alter this.

Artists are another notable local group. Exmoor has always attracted writers and painters, providing inspiration and opportunity: here in Withypool this tradition is alive and thriving. The conversion of a barn at Lanacre into a studio and gallery represents a good example of otherwise unwanted traditional agricultural structures being modified to support newer creative occupations.

With the example of Mike Witney working with others, Sue Wakeham highlighting the benefits of gathering small producers into a larger group with greater marketing potential, and a group of artists working individually yet sharing gallery space, there could well be a model here in Withypool for craftsmen and women producers in rural areas.

Meanwhile all sorts of other people in the village quietly continue to put their skills and training to good use, supplementing farming incomes or pensions through a wide range of activities from chiropractic to information technology, from art work to personal care, from teaching and instructing to journalism and publishing.

And, as we sip our refreshment, we might consider the huge potential of the tourist industry, with its catering, accommodation and other economic opportunities (guiding walks, riding, nature safaris, archaeological projects, traditional sports along with newer activities such as mountain biking, photography, drawing, painting and writing – to name a few) for which Withypool is so well placed, in the heart of Exmoor.

In fact, our journey through the story and around the people and places of Withypool shows that it is far from moribund, and that there is every reason why the village should face a happy, secure and lively future.

Chapter 14

Postscript

No history can ever be complete, certainly not one which deals with a living community. Not only does life itself go on, but there is so much in the present and the past, in living memory as well as in unseen and unheard evidence, that what we capture and record is but a shred, a hint of history.

So we apologise for what we have missed out, very conscious of the many people and the stories we have not had the space or time to include. We hope there will be future opportunities to address this.

However, our wish is that this fragment may give some inkling of the larger story and a flavour of how one event led to one another. In the remembrance of small actions and responses, we may begin to understand larger developments, for in order to consider big events, one has to look at individual experiences.

It was interesting that some people found it hard to believe that it was worth reading, let alone writing, the story of Withypool. But this is where people have lived – and still do – through peace and anxiety, shortages and warfare, upheaval and tranquillity for as many millennia as any, within a little tight knit community itself travelling through experiences which make up our national history.

As we have shown, the story of Withypool – in all its isolation – has involved some unusual, distinguished and celebrated people. But above all this is a story of a village – a place where people worked and played, lived and loved, were born and died. And continue to do so.

The buildings, be they church or bridge, house or farm, change with time; the natural features, the river, the ponies, the moor itself, also quietly alter – yet all live on, all helping to make up the village that we recognise, and would have recognised, were we to travel back centuries.

But what survives pre-eminently, is people – people with the same names, sharing DNA with their forebears, along with the fresh blood of incomers – who make up a small community which embraces all who live and have lived there, and acknowledges their significance.